WITHDRAWN

WITHDRAWN

REFLECTIONS ON AMERICA

BY THE SAME AUTHOR

TRUE HUMANISM, NEW YORK: SCRIBNERS, 1938
(Translation of *Humanisme Intégral*)

RANSOMING THE TIME, NEW YORK: SCRIBNERS, 1941
(Second edition, 1948)

EDUCATION AT THE CROSSROADS, YALE UNIVERSITY PRESS, 1943

MAN AND THE STATE, CHICAGO UNIVERSITY PRESS, 1951

THE RANGE OF REASON, NEW YORK: SCRIBNERS, 1953

CREATIVE INTUITION IN ART AND POETRY, NEW YORK:
PANTHEON, 1953

ON THE PHILOSOPHY OF HISTORY, NEW YORK:
SCRIBNERS, 1957

*

*THE SOCIAL AND POLITICAL PHILOSOPHY
OF JACQUES MARITAIN*, excerpts by JOSEPH W. EVANS AND
LEO R. WARD, NEW YORK: SCRIBNERS, 1955

REFLECTIONS

on

AMERICA

BY

Jacques Maritain

CHARLES SCRIBNER'S SONS

NEW YORK

© COPYRIGHT 1958 BY JACQUES MARITAIN

B–3.58[V]

ALL RIGHTS RESERVED. NO PART OF THIS BOOK
MAY BE REPRODUCED IN ANY FORM WITHOUT
THE PERMISSION OF CHARLES SCRIBNER'S SONS.

PRINTED IN THE UNITED STATES OF AMERICA

LIBRARY OF CONGRESS CATALOG CARD NUMBER 58-5719

917.3
M342r

To

JOHN U. NEF

WHO LOVES MY COUNTRY
AS I LOVE HIS

9525

CONTENTS

7

Contents

Foreword

This little book grew out of three seminars which were held at the University of Chicago, under the auspices of the *Committee on Social Thought,* on November 6th, 7th and 9th, 1956. My talks were stenotyped, and in revising the copy I have added a number of pages, taking care, moreover, in no way to change the original character of my approach. I doubt that I would ever have undertaken to treat of the topic *ex professo.* So it was essential for me to keep in the book the tone of informal, familiar, and desultory conversation that I used originally.

It may happen that some undignified colloquial expressions will be found here and there in my text. Why did I indulge in this kind of vernacular? I no longer wish (as I did in my youth) to irritate the reader, or even to put his sense of humor to the test. But the fact is that I hate a perpetually and uniformly serious style; it is, to my mind, like those *grandes robes de pédants* of which Pascal spoke and in which people's fancy likes to clothe philosophers. I take truth seriously; I don't take myself seriously.

Foreword

I thought it especially advisable to have these "random reflections on the American scene"[1] put forward before an American audience and tested by its reactions and criticisms. I must say that the reactions were most encouraging, and that, except for a few points of detail (such as the role of ideology in American history), the comments of the participants in the seminars were a corroboration of the general accuracy of the views I submitted. I wish to express my gratitude to the audience, and especially to the chairman, Professor John U. Nef, as well as to Saul Alinsky, Professor Yves Simon, Mrs. Russell Davenport, Reverend Father John Egan and Reverend Father Edward O'Connor, whose remarks I particularly appreciated.

I am also indebted to the valuable observations of my friends John Hite, Marshall Suther, E. B. O. and Cornelia Borgerhoff. To all of them my most cordial thanks.

I would like to add three remarks.

In the first place: this book emanates from experiences and convictions which are common to my wife and myself. Her admiration and love for this country are as deep as mine. She has long wished that I might bear this sort of testimony, and she has a great part in it.

[1] This was the original title of my three seminars in Chicago.

In the second place: no allusion to politics is to be found in my talks. It is not, to be sure, that I disregard or ignore the importance of political activity. As I grow old I realize more and more how fundamental for mankind this activity is—and how deeply it depends on the most disappointing contingencies. If I were ever to write on these matters, especially on the matter of international politics, I would have many things to say, and not always flattering, even for the countries I love most. But the subject I had to treat of was quite different, and more appropriate to the only task to which I am now holding fast, which is philosophy. It is by peoples, not by governments, that the attention of a philosopher is captivated.

In the third place: I venture to think that the remarks contained in this book draw a particular significance from the fact that its author is a Frenchman, brought up in the culture and traditions of his country, who looks at the American scene with European eyes—unbiased, I hope, European eyes—and who, privileged enough to have been accepted as part and parcel of today's American cultural life, is all the more at ease in uniting love for America and love for France in his inmost affections as he sees between the French people and the American people, however profoundly different from one another they may be, a mysterious affinity, a strange and deep-rooted congeniality, which make their historical destinies convergent.

*

Random as they may be, the remarks submitted in this book are not without some internal order. They are, in actual fact, divided into three groups. The attentive reader will have no difficulty in discerning the reasons for this grouping. Yet it is perhaps better to give some explanation of my own, and to make clear that the first group, composed of Chapters I to VIII, deals with things which are more obvious or more immediately apparent. The second group, composed of Chapters IX to XIV, deals with things which are more difficult to grasp because they relate to aspects more deep-seated in the soul; and the third group (Chapters XV to XX) deals with things which, to my mind, are also of crucial significance, but which have especially to do with the realm of social and cultural life, and with American institutions.

These three groups of reflections are linked by a melodic thread, if I may so put it, which passes from Chapter II to Chapter XIII and Chapter XIX.

May I be permitted to add that in writing these pages I have tried to submit a great variety of remarks to the golden rule of brevity. This book was not made to be read in a hurry. If it is read at leisure, it will perhaps appear not completely useless.

I

I

By Way of a Preface

Though for a long time I have wished to speak about this country and give expression to my admiration for it, it was not without much hesitation that I chose the topic of these talks.

First, because when you live a long time in a country you get more and more information about it; and the more information you get, the more confused you become, information blurring more or less your personal experience and disclosing the infinite complexity and ceaselessly contrasting aspects of so vast a human reality.

Secondly, because my philosophical work prevented me from undertaking any systematic, complete and supposedly "scientific" study of this matter.

Yet, on the one hand, I felt a growing inner urge to bear witness to this country and to its people—it is a matter of justice and of gratitude for me. And in this respect I am only playing my small part in a French tradition which began with Chateaubriand and Tocqueville.

On the other hand, I came to realize that however

helpful and necessary systematic surveys and scientific analyses may be, as, for instance, Gunnar Myrdal's book, *An American Dilemma,* on the condition of the colored people, there is room, nevertheless, for quite a different approach, a merely personal, experiential, non-scientific approach, which has a good chance of being as true, in its own way, as the scientific and objective one, and even of disclosing deeper, though less firmly established, truths.

For in the last analysis, our appreciation of a country or a people has to do with the knowledge of the individual, of the singular, of that immense collective personality which is a people with its history, its mores, its common psyche, its dreams, its vocation. And most important in the knowledge of the singular is what cannot be demonstrated, and depends on a kind of experience and perception so rooted in individual instances, in person to person relationships, that the statements in which it is expressed cannot be *explained* or *proved* by universal notions and rational disquisition.

The fact remains that in trying to express my reflections on the American scene, my position will be quite vulnerable: precisely because my statements will be susceptible of no demonstration. Moreover, they will claim to constitute neither an historical analysis nor any kind of complete picture, nor any kind of "explanation." They will leave aside many important questions for the discussion of which my impromptu way of speaking was not suitable. They will be incomplete, subjective, disconnected—random reflections. Moreover, in such matters there is always a certain margin of error regarding the bearing of our observations, accurate as they may be.

But, for all that, I am confident that there are true insights at the core of my random reflections. Furthermore, the truths they contain are most valuable for me, for they are in essence a statement of why I love America, that America which I have known for almost a quarter of a century.

I am aware of the fact that every great human reality is ambivalent, and that the best things involve dangers or are accompanied by more or less serious defects. I am aware, too, of the severity with which Americans, and the best among them, criticize certain aspects of their own culture and nation. I shall have some opportunities to point out, myself, several of those unfavorable aspects. What matters to me is that they are of small import in comparison with all that I love in this country, all that which makes it crucially important for the hopes of mankind and the future of civilization.

These preliminary remarks were destined to make clear the nature and purpose of the seminar out of which grew this book. In particular they make clear, I hope, why I have tried to cling to my own personal experience, and to forget the books, the very good books, which I have read on the matter, such as Tocqueville's, André Siegfried's, Gilbert Chinard's *La Doctrine de l'Américanisme,* Waldo Frank's *The New Discovery of America,* John Nef's *The United States and Civilization,* Elinor Nef's *Letters and Notes,* Yves Simon's *La Civilisation Américaine,* and also those which I have on my desk but have not yet read, such as Jacques Barzun's *God's Country and Mine,* and Max Lerner's *America as a Civilization.*

II

First Impressions

I think that as a rule first impressions are particularly valuable. Of course they contain an element of chance. They may be wrong. Georges Duhamel, for instance, had bad luck—he could not forgive America for the thermometer that an Immigration doctor forcibly put into his mouth upon his arrival on these shores. But leaving aside accidental interferences and assuming that the traveller is sufficiently open-minded, his first impressions about a new country may be superficial and oversimplified—they are, for all that, generally revealing, loaded with significant insight.

With respect to this country, a more particular remark may be added. There are many foreign travellers who are not biased—who even are good and clear-sighted observers, capable of sound, cool practical judgment. They appreciate America, and they like her. They weigh the pros and cons, and they conclude by admiring this country a great deal, with some suitable restraint, to be sure, a certain number of prudent qualifications, and sometimes, in addition, some good and more or less patronizing advice.

And, there are other foreign travellers who are struck right away with what we call in French *le coup de foudre,* love at first sight. Love at first sight does not deal with an *object,* but with a *person.* For those whom it strikes it is like a sudden illumination into a deep-rooted secret. They have been initiated.

This is so true that a friend of mine—a great French scholar—who underwent, as I did, this kind of experience, likes to think of the Frenchmen who got in this way, at one stroke, some inner understanding of this country, as constituting a group of privileged people, a sort of club, in which each one is on brotherly terms with the others by reason of the common understanding in question.

Now the very fact of which I am speaking—love at first sight—has its own significance. I would say that it takes place more frequently with respect to France and America than with respect to any other country. Contrary to Pascal's saying, we don't love qualities, we love persons; sometimes by reason of their defects as well as of their qualities. When he who, meeting for the first time either France or America, falls in love at first sight, it is because he is confronted with a moral personality, a moral vocation, something of invaluable dignity, which is spiritual in nature, and which, I think, in the last analysis is quickened, in one way or another, by some spark of the Christian spirit and legacy.

*

What was, then, my own first impression?

It was quite definite, though difficult to express in words. I felt I was obscurely confronted with a deep-seated contrast of immense bearing, a sharp, far-reaching contrast between *the people* on the one hand, and, on the other hand, what I would like to call the externally superimposed *structure or ritual of civilization*.

What I call the structure or ritual of civilization was the industrial civilization, born in Europe and arrived here from abroad, which I saw in this first insight as hanging over a people of pioneers and free men under God.

This industrial civilization, which I had learned to know in Europe, appeared to me, here, both as gigantically developed (like many things trans-planted from Europe over here) and as a kind of ritual dedicated to some foreign goddess. Its inner logic, as I knew it—originally grounded as it was on the principle of the fecundity of money and the absolute primacy of individual profit—was, every-where in the world, inhuman and materialist.

But, by a strange paradox, the people who lived and toiled under this structure or ritual of civilization were keeping their own souls apart from it. At least as regards the essentials, their souls and vital energy, their dreams, their everyday effort, their idealism and generosity, were running against the grain of the inner logic of the superimposed structure. They were freedom-loving and mankind-loving people, people clinging to the importance of ethical standards, anxious to save the world, the most humane and the least materialist among modern peoples which had reached the industrial stage.

Thus the basic thing in my first impression was the sharp distinction to be made between the spirit of the American people and the logic of the superimposed structure or ritual of civilization: and not only the distinction, but the state of tension, of hidden conflict, between this spirit of the people and this logic of the structure; the steady, latent rebellion of the spirit of the people against the logic of the structure.

Then a telling question arose: what will be the result of the conflict between the spirit of the people and the logic of the structure? This was the second basic element of my first impression.

Of course, this first impression made things a little too simplified, too dramatized. But I think it was fundamentally true. And, as a matter of fact, I came over for the first time in 1933, at the time, it seems to me, of a drastic turning point in the very drama which had begun years ago with Theodore Roosevelt.

And the more I lived in this country, the more I realized that the answer to the question I just mentioned was: the spirit of the people is gradually overcoming and breaking the logic of the structure.

In other words, the vital, pragmatic, completely unsystematic pressure exercised by the American people and the American soul on the structures of our modern industrial civilization is transforming from within the inner dynamism and historical trends of the industrial regime. It is causing this regime to pass beyond capitalism. The people have thus vanquished the inner logic of the industrial regime considered in its first historical phase, and have, almost without knowing it, inaugurated a really new phase in modern civilization.

I only mention this point now. I will discuss it at greater length in a further chapter.

III

Deliverance from History

The title of this chapter represents another aspect of my first impressions.

During my first visit to New York I was invaded by a kind of thrilling enthusiasm and pleasure in the sudden feeling that here we are freed from history. For a European long immersed in all the rotten stuff of past events, past hatreds, past habits, past glories and past diseases which compose a sort of over-whelming historical heredity, the first contact with America is thus liable to produce a sort of intoxica-tion, a delight in a new-born freedom, as if the old burden of historical necessities were suddenly put aside. It seemed that everything is possible to human freedom.

Of course, this sentiment that one is freed from history is a great illusion. We are never freed from history. But the illusion points, I think, to a very significant fact: this country is entirely turned toward the future, not toward the past. An appeal of this kind, a suction so to speak, exercised by the future upon the whole nation to such a degree and with such power, is in my opinion something new in human history, and is no doubt an element of the greatness of America.

You are not freed from your own history. On the contrary, you are deeply attached to it, even to the point of cherishing pieces of colonial furniture, and of artificially maintaining at great cost villages equipped and functioning as in the eighteenth century. But in one sense you are freed from the history of your European ancestors, for you have voluntarily cut off your links with this history. You depend, as does every Western man, on the history of Europe. But this history is your pre-history.

And your own history as a people, as a nation, is quite recent. It is barely two hundred years old. You have not had time for hardening, for sclerosis. And the voice of your Founding Fathers still appeals to your emotions in a lively manner (I would say that for the average Frenchman the *Déclaration des Droits de l'Homme* is an old piece of parchment, but for you the Declaration of Independence seems to have been written some fifty years ago).

In this sense—and in this sense only—the American people are young. On the one hand, they enjoy that bloom, that openness to the future, which Aristotle called the flower of youth. On the other hand, there is in them a certain lack of that collective, common experience as a nation, which is an advantage, sometimes dearly paid for, of the Old World.

With respect to the illusory but telling sentiment of being freed from history, I would like to submit another remark—relating to the root incompatibility which exists between the American people and Marxist philosophy. For Marx, history is, as you know, an immense and terrible set of concatenated necessities, in the bosom of which man slaves toward his final emancipation. When he becomes at last, through communism, master of his own history, then he will drive the chariot of Juggernaut which had previously crushed him. But for the American people it is quite another story. They are not interested in driving the chariot of Juggernaut. They have gotten rid of Juggernaut. It is not in any future messianic freedom of mankind, nor in mastering the necessities of history, it is in man's present freedom that they are interested. And as Diogenes proved movement, so they prove this freedom in walking. History is, in one sense, behind them. They walk, they march, they gambol ahead of history, as in those big processions with resounding bands and girls in fancy dress, which so often enliven American streets.

IV

The Old Tag of American Materialism

I have spoken of my first impressions on arriving in this country. Since that time I have come to realize more and more the immensity of the human effort which was brought into play to create a new world within the course of two centuries, to give to half a continent a material and moral equipment fit to free men and to build a civilization really and genuinely original in character, capable of astonishing, captivating and seducing the hearts of men.

And I have more and more admired both the creative work which was thus accomplished and the process of self-creation through which it unceasingly continues.

I have already said that the American people are the least materialist among the modern peoples which have attained the industrial stage. As I put it in a parting talk [1] before leaving for Rome in 1945, "ce pays n'est pas un pays matérialiste comme le disent trop volontiers certains Américains eux-

1. At a lunch given by the French American Club, New York, March 15th, 1945. In *Pour la Justice*, New York: Maison Française, 1945, p. 358.

mêmes, il se fraye a force de courage un chemin difficile où la liberté de l'homme doit soulever le poids de matérialisme que la civilisation moderne, avec sa tendance à la technocratie et à l'hégémonie de l'argent, fait partout peser sur la personne humaine." I would like to insist on this point, because few things, to my mind, are as sickening as the stock remarks with which so many persons in Europe, who are themselves far from despising the earthly goods of this world, reproach this country with its so-called materialism. The power of this fable is so great that sometimes you yourselves are taken in by it. I remember some American ladies in New York who said to me, with a disillusioned (perhaps slightly treacherous) wink: "We are a materialist nation, aren't we?" Well, all this talk about American materialism is no more than a curtain of silly gossip and slander.

In a number of my fellow Europeans the fable in question proceeds from an old prejudice, confusing spirituality with an aristocratic contempt for any improvement in material life (especially the material life of others). In other cases the fable of American materialism (seemingly corroborated, as it is, by some of your exports, like average Hollywood productions) appears as a kind of compensation for the frustrations Europe has endured, and a kind of solace for the agony which the fact of owing gratitude to another imposes on human nature. And in other cases, it results, contrariwise, from too great an expectation, from the fact that Europeans expect from you an understanding which they fail sometimes to obtain.

*

I have no intention of denying that in America as in all other places in the world, especially among industrialized nations, large areas in the common consciousness—the most obvious, as a rule, and the most superficial areas—have been infected by the miasmata that emanate from the structures and ritual of our modern civilization; the noise made by a crowd of vulgar assertions, which measure everything either in terms of statistics and facts and figures or in terms of success, fun, and practical power, hold "ideas" to be only something to be "sold" to a possible consumer, silent partner, or sucker, and see human conduct as a by-product either of hormones or of economic factors—this noise is too great not to be heard.

The observer may be misled, it is true, especially when it comes to the answers given by people about their personal aims in life, or about their political choices, by the appearances and facilities of language,

I mean by the fact that as a rule, in our everyday life, we use words in a way which will save our brain cells as much work as possible—and it is much easier and less expensive, in this respect, to have recourse to mean rather than to lofty platitudes. Yet the universal diffusion of a kind of popularized, anonymous positivistic philosophy, to which pragmatist dynamism, in this country, gave higher intellectual standing and additional pep, can only make more real and more insidious the process of materialist contagion of which I am speaking.

I don't deny these things; I do say that to invoke them as a proof of so-called American materialism is to talk nonsense. For, in the first place, they are in no way specifically American; exactly the same symptoms, in relation to similar sociological or psychological areas, leap to the eye everywhere (especially in Europe) where the industrial regime and its congenial ideological fumes are prevalent; only the vocal expression seems perhaps to be a little cruder and more naive here, whereas elsewhere it is either more cautious and sophisticated or more elaborately cynical.

And, in the second place, there are here plenty of other, utterly opposing trends and characteristics, which relate to much deeper and more significant strata in the common psyche, and which are typically American, and give the lie to the fable of American materialism.

*

Well, I would like to ask the European critics of this country what are in their eyes the criteria of materialism. Are perhaps generosity and good will the signs of a materialistic cast of mind? Speaking not of such or such an individual, of course, but of the general cast of mind and the collective trends and customs of the people, what I know is that the basic characteristics of the American people are generosity, good will, the sense of human fellowship.

There are, of course, egoistic individuals in America as everywhere, but America is not egoist; for the common consciousness of America, egoism is shameful.

There are greedy individuals in America as there are everywhere, but there is no avarice in the American cast of mind.

The American people are neither squeamish nor hypocritical about the importance of money in the modern world. Even their frank admission of this importance makes Europeans uncomfortable. For

33

the average European cares about money as well as the average American, but he tries to conceal the fact, for he has been accustomed to associating money with avarice.

Here, on the contrary, money is cared for openly, because money is considered a means, and must not be kept but rather spent—for improving one's own life, to be sure, and one's freedom of action, but also, and this is fundamental, for improving the lives and freedom of others.

Americans like to give. Of course, there is the exemption from taxes for gifts directed to the common welfare; but this very law about taxes would not have been possible if the astute legislator did not know that as a rule the American people are aware of the fact that it is better to give than to receive. Not only the great foundations,[1] but the ordinary course of activity of American institutions and the innumerable American private groups show us that

1. I have carping-minded friends who insist that the system has its flaws. People, they say, who might have started at their own risk some work which would be genuinely original or would genuinely answer certain definite needs, sometimes wait for the mouthful of a grant, like gaping chicks, before undertaking anything (any project so conceived as to have a chance of being successfully applied). I don't know whether there is an element of truth in such a criticism. In any case it has to do with quite accidental drawbacks, and the great American foundations, born of freedom and immune from State control, are one of the most noble and beneficial institutions in modern culture.

34

the ancient Greek and Roman idea of the *civis praeclarus,* the dedicated citizen who spends his money in the service of the common good, plays an essential part in American consciousness. And let me observe that more often than not the gifts in question are made for the sake of education and knowledge. Frequently people who were unable to have a college education make large gifts to universities.

There is no materialism, I think, in the astonishing, countless initiatives of fraternal help which are the daily bread of the American people, or in the profound feeling of obligation toward others which exists in them, especially toward any people abroad who are in distress.

I shall never forget the work of the rescue committees for European scholars which I witnessed during the war, and all those luncheons which crowds of people eagerly attended in order to have an eloquent auctioneer, at dessert time, extract big checks from their pockets. I shall never forget the admirable devotion with which Alvin Johnson, then President of the New School for Social Research, pursued this work of rescue, nor the fraternal cooperation he extended to our French-speaking *École Libre des Hautes Études* when it was created with the help and on the premises of the New School.

There is no materialism in the fact that the American charities, drawing money from every purse, and notably to assist people abroad, run every year into such enormous sums that charity ranks among the largest American industries, the second or third in size, according to statisticians.

Yes, yes, I know, the very fact involves a certain danger that charity itself will become industrialized, or overorganized. Well, people who sit on their money like brooding hens are certain to avoid that danger! And if the collection of money for the needy and the helpless is so well organized here that in giving our contribution automatically each year, we may be tempted to think that we are excused from ever giving our heart (but can we believe that European streets are jammed with people busy giving their hearts?), let us not forget what an immense amount of personal attention to one's neighbor and what personal effort is unceasingly put forth in all the groups which exist in this country, and which spring up every day, to meet some particular human misfortune or some particular social maladjustment.

*

I would like to mention now other characteristics of American life, namely, the extraordinary resilience and versatility with which the American people face new problems and adjust themselves to new situations. They don't like to accept things as they are, and to let people shift for themselves by dint of suffering and ingenuity. They prefer to change things and situations. They prefer to find a new arrangement, new equipment, a new gadget, a new line of social activity, for the sake of the human individuals involved. Now, did not Hegel speak of the "infinite elasticity" of the spirit? Such resilience is a sign of a perpetual alertness of the spirit acting as a ferment in the mass.

Let us say, and this seems quite typical to me, that in the immense population of America there is no stagnation. As a result, I don't see America as a mainland, but as a sea, a big ocean. Sometimes a storm arises, a formidable current develops, and it seems it will engulf everything. Wait a moment, another current will appear and bring the first one to naught. A great country, with as many windshifts as the sea.[1]

At the origin of this *fluidity* there is the activity of the mind at work in the people, in the humble ways of daily life.

1. May I note in this connection that it would perhaps be a good idea for official propaganda not to seem regularly to ignore the various dissenting currents, the conflicts and oppositions, the more or less adventurous reforming enterprises, which are a sign of American vitality.

37

Many other aspects might be stressed. First, I shall point out the concern of the American people for moral and religious values, their attitude toward moral conscience. I do not say that they always act according to the dictates of conscience—what nation does? I say that they feel miserable, they endure terrible discomfort when they have a guilty conscience. The very fact alone of nursing a doubt as to whether their conduct was or was not ethically irreproachable causes them pain. The result is sometimes unexpected, as the wave of fondness for the Japanese people which developed after Hiroshima. Let us say that hiring the devil for help will never be agreeable even to your politicians. The common consciousness of this country loathes cynicism, cannot be cynical.

A second aspect is the fundamental part played in this country by free discussion, involving that right to dissent without which there is no community of free men, and which no historical circumstance can impair here for long. There is a perpetual process of self-examination and self-criticism going on everywhere and in every sphere of American life: a phenomenon incomprehensible without a quest for truth of which a materialist cast of mind is incapable.

A third aspect is the great battle which is being fought in the educational field to develop the humanities,[1] the liberal arts, philosophy, and to make wisdom the final aim, a battle of which the members of the Committee on Social Thought are especially aware. It is in this so-called materialist country that professors of classics, each in his own great or small college, struggle with unequalled devotion to maintain the intellectual tradition with which they are entrusted; that a strenuous effort is being made by the universities, and by technological institutes as well, to overcome the dangers of overspecialization and the trends toward technocracy which are natural to industrial civilization; and that a reformer of such stature as Robert M. Hutchins has raised his bitter criticisms and insisted on the necessity for intellectual integration—inspiring or prodding in actual fact the vast academic effort of which I just spoke, though naturally his name is too well known to the public ever to be mentioned on campuses.

1. From among the great scholars who are representing in the United States the tradition of the highest humanistic culture, I would like to mention and pay my personal tribute of admiration to Mark Van Doren, Lane Cooper, Whitney J. Oates, Erwin Panofsky, Huntington Cairns, R. P. Blackmur, Francis Fergusson, who was the first director of Princeton University's Seminars in Literary Criticism, and E. B. O. Borgerhoff, who succeeded him in the direction of the Seminars (Christian Gauss Seminars in Criticism).

A fourth aspect is the thirst, the eagerness for knowledge—not only with a view to its practical applications, but first of all as a vital necessity for the mind—which I have had the opportunity to observe, year after year, in American youth everywhere in the country. Such a thirst exists in the people as a whole, in uneducated as in educated persons. Here as elsewhere it is not created by education and teachers (sometimes they seem rather anxious to kill it). It is a need of nature, particularly fresh, huge and intense in the American people.

A fifth aspect is the thirst for spiritual life which is deep in the American soul, and the signs of which are more and more manifest, especially among young people. In a number of people it is more or less unconscious, more or less repressed by the conditions of existence and the tyranny of unceasing activity. For all that it is real and alive, and exercises continual pressure on souls.

For many years I was aware of this fact; I am particularly pleased to have laid stress on it at a time when such views seemed more than paradoxical, and my Carthusian friends in Europe told me that the very idea of ever having a Charterhouse in America was completely ridiculous.

In a lecture on Action and Contemplation written

some twenty years ago,[1] I insisted that there were in America great reserves and possibilities for contemplation; the activism which is to the fore appears, I said, in many cases as a remedy against despair, and masks a hidden aspiration to contemplation. I saw in the American inclination to be moved by large idealistic feelings an effect of this hidden aspiration. And I concluded: "The cult of action is not specifically American. It is a European idea, an idea of post-Renaissance and post-Reformation Europe. What may mislead us in this matter, so it seems to me, is that the New Continent, with terrible loyalty, has taken some of the Old World's ideas, transplanted into virgin soil, and carried them to their limits. When in America some few come to realize better the value of contemplative activity, its superiority and fecundity, I believe the possibilities I have spoken of will manifest themselves, at least in a small way, but forcefully enough gradually to modify the general scheme of values."

Well, now Tom Merton's books are best-sellers, great classical works on spiritual life are published in abundance and are widely read in the most varied

1. This lecture, given in the United States in 1938, was published later as Chapter VII in my book *Scholasticism and Politics*, New York: Macmillan, 1940. Used with the permission of The Macmillan Company.

circles, the Trapp of Gethsemani alone has more novices than all European Trapps combined, and is obliged to multiply new foundations; the monasteries founded by various contemplative Orders are so crowded that they refuse candidates for lack of room; and there is a Charterhouse in this country.

*

I have pointed out a certain number of aspects of American life which seem to me to be typical. I could continue in the same vein. There is no end to the enumeration of the various features peculiar, quite peculiar indeed, to so-called *American materialism.*

Let me only add that from *Moby Dick* and *The Scarlet Letter* to *Look Homeward, Angel* and *Requiem for a Nun*—from Edgar Allan Poe and Emily Dickinson to Hart Crane, Allen Tate and T. S. Eliot (who has remained an American in spite of himself)—American literature, in its most objectively careful scrutinies, has been preoccupied with the beyond and the nameless which haunt our blood. Man, as it sees him, is a restless being gropingly, sometimes miserably, at grips with his fleshly condition—whom obviously no kind of materialist paradise can ever satisfy.

V

A Few Vulnerable Points

Let us now discuss a few vulnerable points.

The first one I shall mention is by no means a weakness. It is a deeply human and noble characteristic. I am alluding to the fact that the American people are anxious to have their country loved; they need to be loved. (You will never find such a need in an Englishman. As to Frenchmen, they are so sure in advance that everybody loves them that they don't feel any particular anxiety about the matter. But they are very much shocked when they realize it is not true.) Well, this desire to have America loved is the mark of a soul which lies open to the sense of human brotherhood; it plays an important part, I think, in the general psychology of this country.

I do not forget that the cultivated American—perhaps because he feels a particular urge to cast a critical eye in a national environment he considers uncritical—is as anxious to have America criticized as to have her loved. As a result, any writer who bitterly denounces the vices of this country is listened to with special care and sorrowful appreciation;

though he hurts, and is gently packed off to the *tenebrae exteriores* where he belongs. And the writer who admires and praises this country has the nice qualities of a gratifying friend, to be sure, but is considered softheaded. The love of Americans for their country is not an indulgent, it is an exacting and chastising love; they cannot tolerate its defects. Frenchmen behave in the same way, yet they carp at their fellow Frenchmen with fun, either sarcastic or cheerful, whereas Americans denigrate America with ethical melancholy.

*

Now, in the second place: I remember that, speaking of his fellow Americans, especially of American youth, a great friend of mine said to me one day: *"They have no roots."*

The worst scoundrel in Europe has roots; there is some old human legacy to which he can stick, for better or for worse. Here there is, it seems to me, a certain instability, or fleetingness, in the life of individuals; one is less sure that "it will last," that they will carry through, I don't say with the job they are determined to do, I would rather say with the inner purpose they have formed as to the direction of their own personal life.

That is why, among the general features of American psychology, and despite many exceptions, of course, I think we can observe a certain proneness to a peculiar sort of impatience, and, as a result, a proneness also to quick discouragement. Let me make my thought clearer. I just said that the impatience in question is a peculiar sort of impatience. American crowds (when waiting for a train, for instance, or inconvenienced by any of the multiple regulations of our modern life, or plagued by red tape) are incomparably more patient than French crowds. Men and women in this country confront suffering with great courage, and often a strange Stoic resignation. In emergencies they manifest admirable endurance. But they are not patient with life.

They are not patient with their own life, as a rule. And they get disturbed and discouraged very soon, if the work they have undertaken is slow to succeed. The American artist, the American painter, would like to have his work satisfy him rapidly and give immediate results, whereas a French painter, a Cézanne, a Rouault—disregarded, spurned by all for perhaps thirty or forty years—remains bent on working with furious patience. As a rule, I think, a young American would be afraid that such an atti-

tude marked only presumptuous stubbornness. If
he is not recognized, he starts doubting himself. He
thinks he is a failure.

*

The third point I would like to mention is akin to
the second. It is a kind of inner insecurity—masked,
of course, by forced optimism. I don't believe very
much in that big, radiant optimism which social
etiquette obliges American faces to display. It masks
more often than not worry and inner insecurity.

In actual fact, the great idea is to do *as if* evil did
not exist. There was indeed, at one time, a real philosophy of the negation of evil in this country. War
has put an end to it. American youth knows now
that evil exists, that death exists, that the devil exists.
This fact, at all events, does not diminish the inner
insecurity of which I am speaking.

I deeply respect this inner insecurity, inner discomfort, repressed anxiety—these things to which
many people are a prey. For they are proof that one
does not bluff oneself, that one is aware of the awful
magnitude and complexity of the problems in which
human life is entangled. I believe, nevertheless, that
in the last analysis they are caused by a lack of sufficiently firm and integrated intellectual certainties.

Be that as it may, the fact is that people here need

often to be intellectually reassured; to know more unquestionably, either through better established rational convictions, or through the testimony of their fellow men, that they are right, especially as regards their idealistic incentives and their faith in the power of good will and generosity.

As a corollary, I would say that the unjust European (and Asian) refusal to recognize the good intentions of this country, while trying to offer of the immense effort of American good will any kind of cheap cynical explanation, is of a nature to cause damage to the American soul itself.

*

Finally, a fourth point relates to the fact that Americans need, as it were, their natural environment to be themselves. That is probably why the behavior of Americans abroad is so different from their behavior at home.

I was able to observe the fact in France and in Italy. My Parisian friends had the same impression. Most of the Americans they had known in this country did not seem to be the same persons in Europe.

When they are abroad it seems that they feel unhappy, afraid of meeting people, shy. And, as a result, they tend to become arrogant. Where are their cordial, genial, cheerful manners? They left

47

them behind, in the native climate of the big country. One is led to think that each individual needs his home, his natural environment so much that abroad he feels estranged from himself.

VI

The Race Question

Except for friendly relations with various colored persons whom I highly esteem and appreciate, I have not had an opportunity, in my own personal experience, to confront the race question in America. I know of it by hearsay—a great deal of hearsay indeed. This question, moreover, has historical and sociological roots which make it much too complex to be discussed in a few pages. The following remarks are not a discussion of it, but rather a few reflections apropos of it.

The most general fact concerning the race question in America is the opposition which exists between the mores and the law—I mean to say, between the feelings and behavior of large parts of the white population, and the Federal law. Just as, at the time of Lincoln, the Federal government opposed slavery, to the point where the nation became involved in a tragic civil war, so the Federal law, in all matters which depend on it, stands for the complete equality of all citizens, without any sort of racial discrimination. And thus, each time an open conflict

49

between the mores and the Federal law occurs, a kind of showdown takes place.

Furthermore, it is relevant, it seems to me, to distinguish between two categories of problems: on the one hand those which have to do with civil rights and legal segregation, and on the other hand those which have to do with racial prejudice in individual relations.

*

Segregation enforced by law, in its multifarious forms pervading all aspects of social life, still exists in Southern states, as a legacy of a social structure which was based on slavery. It corresponds not only to ingrained prejudices, but also to ingrained customs and traditions to which the daily activities of the white man and the Negro have been adjusted for generations, and in the framework of which better conditions for the Negro population, and even progress toward a kind of paternalist racial justice, were able to develop—on the assumed condition that Negroes should continue being regarded, and regarding themselves, as socially under age.

One must, no doubt, look with understanding and sympathy at the difficulties with which many men of good will, who are aware of their duties toward colored people, but bound by their own local traditions, are confronted in the South. It is quite possible, moreover, that (just as was the case before the Civil War, under the regime of slavery) a number of Negro families may lead a happier (more care-free) life under the afore-mentioned circumstances than they will with the responsibilities of adult age. Yet the question is not a question of happiness, but of human right. And it is inescapable.

I have no doubt that after a more or less long interval, and despite the obstacles which certain local elements may put in the way, legal segregation will completely disappear, under the double pressure of Federal legislation and the decisions of the Supreme Court, and of the fight conducted with such poise, dignity, and self-devotion by the Negro population in Southern states. At this point I would like to pay my tribute of admiration to the colored people of Montgomery, Alabama, and their spiritual leader, Reverend Martin Luther King. They gave, in the famous bus boycott of 1956, an example whose historic importance may be considerable—the most striking example as yet seen in this country of a possible use, in the Occident, of Gandhian methods of non-violence.

*

As regards the second category of problems, those which deal with racial prejudice in individual relations, they are not limited to the Southland; to one extent or another they are problems for the whole nation. Miss Margaret Mead [1] observes that the American soldiers who fraternized with the Manus had no anti-Negro feeling with respect to the Negro race in general, to Negroes in the world, but could very well nurture strong anti-Negro bias with respect to *their own* colored people, *their own* Negroes in America: for then it is a question of tensions and competition within the social group, and of the presence of a supposedly alien element in the community. The demons of the human heart are ready to feed on the opportunity.

It is not only in the South, but also in any place in the North where a large afflux of Negro population takes place, especially highly industrialized areas, that the popular prejudice against colored people is rampant, composed as it is of a mixture of fear, a contemptuous superiority complex, and pleasure in humiliating and bullying others, with a latent possibility of awakening here and there the worst instincts of destruction and persecution; it was in the suburbs of Chicago that, some years ago, particularly hateful violence was used to prevent Negro families from moving into sections inhabited by white people. I don't speak of the restricted hotels, restricted clubs,

1. See *infra,* pp. 68–69.

or restricted beaches, and of the "correct" forms that racial prejudice is taking in some parts of the educated or well-to-do strata of the population (and not only in relation to colored people, but in relation to Jews, and sometimes to Irishmen as well . . .).

*

These things are heart-rending, and lead now and then to abominable excesses like lynching; this country will probably take a much longer time to put an end to them than to legal segregation. It will put an end to them, though; because it is determined to do so.

They are a plague on it, and they are incompatible with its spirit, the sense of human fellowship inherent in its people, and the very tenets in which living together is founded here. It may be remarked at this point that one may happen to hear in certain circles, as an attempt to seek some sort of moral alibi, blatant assertions about the so-called inferiority of Negroes; yet nothing resembling a racist doctrine exists in America. As a rule, those who fall prey to racial prejudice do not glory in it; they seem rather to feel uncomfortable about it—it's a kind of physical condition with which they were born, they cannot help feeling this way, that's all. At the bottom of their hearts they realize that they can neither explain nor justify their bias, and consequently they invest it with the mysterious inevitability of a fact of nature.

Another remark may be made, relating to the fact that, whether one likes it or not, Negro citizens are in actual existence an integral part of the nation—in wartime they are called, as any other citizen is, to imperil their lives for it. In becoming "integrated," they are only becoming socially and culturally what they already are existentially. "Negro people have made greater cultural, educational and social progress in a shorter time than has any other ethnic group in recorded history." [1] In proportion as the number of educated Negroes occupying positions of responsibility in the community grows, the very progress toward complete integration gains momentum automatically.

I just said that the American nation is determined to make an end of anti-Negro prejudice with its typically un-American retinue of human inequity, humiliation and sanctioned distress. A sign of this is the persistent urge, stronger than any shuffling which may occur, which leads those elements in the nation officially *representative* of it—namely the legislative and executive branches of the Federal government—to take an always clearer and firmer

1. J. B. Gremillion, *The Journal of a Southern Pastor.*

stand on the matter. Another sign is the progressive awakening of public opinion, as well as the determination and activity of those self-organized groups of good citizens which are, so to speak, the nerve system of the nation. Last, and not least, no decisive victory over feelings and passions rooted in the obscure recesses of human nature can be achieved without profound inner changes caused by the power of spiritual energies. In this regard the role played by the religious organizations is crucial, and so is their responsibility. It is hard to condone the timorous inertia that Catholic as well as Protestant communities showed in the past with respect to the requirements of the Gospel as far as the Negro question was concerned. The very idea of separate pews in churches, and racial segregation at the communion table, is an intolerable shock for the mind. Well, things are changing fast. The uncompromising stand that Archbishop Rummel has taken in Louisiana in behalf of racial equality has unmistakable significance. As a matter of fact, the Protestant and Catholic clergy are now irrevocably engaged in the fight against segregation and racial prejudice. Every Catholic (and many a non-Catholic too) is indebted to the work pursued in this field for more than thirty years by Father John La Farge, and to the steady effort through which his wisdom and courage have

illumined the public mind on the matter.[1] I have
been acquainted with Father La Farge's achievements for a long time, and I am one of his many
admirers. The following sentence from a book, *The
Journal of a Southern Pastor,* recently published by
another priest who shares in his inspiration, has a
universal bearing, as far as Christian conscience is
concerned: "We Catholics," the author writes, "must
deliberately move forward the complete integration
of the Negro, welcoming him as our brother in
Christ and fellow son of God in all the areas of our
society." [2]

*

To sum up, what we witness when we consider in
a general way the race question in America, is the

1. I would like to mention this fundamental book, John La Farge,
The Race Question and the Negro, New York: Longmans, Green, 1943.
As regards recent progress toward integration, cf. the remarkable
report by Harold Fleming and David Loth, *Integration, North and
South,* New York: Meridian Books, 1956. See also Joseph P. Lyford,
"Race Relations Improve," in *America,* April 20, 1957.

2. J. B. Gremillion, *The Journal of a Southern Pastor,* Chicago: Fides
Publishers, 1957, p. 276.—Let me quote a few other lines from the same
book: " 'Well, Father, what are you aiming at? Why did you invite
those colored folks for a meeting here? Are you trying to break down
the wall of segregation?'

" 'Sure, I'm trying to destroy segregation.'

" 'You don't mean you are for social equality, too!'

" 'Sure I am. I have frequently Negro friends in for dinner at
the Rectory . . .

" 'We're having a meeting tomorrow night—Negroes and whites
together . . . And about segregation in church, several years ago I

spectacle of a nation which struggles doggedly against itself, or, more accurately, against large segments of its own people, against a certain legacy of evil in its own mores, and against the demons of the human heart—in order to free itself of abuses which are repellent to its own spirit, and to raise its entire practical behavior to the level of the tenets and principles in which it believes and in the strength of which it was born.

The Negro question is a thorn in the flesh of the American nation. The way in which the nation as such, or the body politic, in the midst of all kinds of local entanglements, reacts against this wound and goes ahead seeking more or less gropingly, but without respite, justice and fairness for all, deserves respect and evinces, within human infirmity, much human grandeur.

---

instructed the ushers to seat Negroes anywhere in Church and preferably *not* in the back pews . . .'

"We must understand the irrational in man. Only radical Christianity can root out this irrational element . . ." (pp. 44-46).

And he goes on to say: "South of the Mason and Dixon line in this area stretching between Louisiana and Virginia there reside one and one-half million Catholics. But more than half of these Catholics, eight hundred thousand, reside in south Louisiana. The pattern of justice or injustice, of Christian love or racial heresy, the pattern established here will affect irrevocably the whole Southland, the whole nation, the whole world . . ." (p. 275).

VII

Another Thorn in the Flesh

The sex question in America is surely no less complicated than the race question. What might elucidate it a little would be an extensive study written by a team of experts, especially a psychologist, an anthropologist, a sociologist, and a philosopher—all of them guided, one would hope, by a genuinely philosophical inspiration.

As for myself, I pretend in no way—no more than in the case of the race question—to offer a complete discussion of the matter in a short chapter. But the problem exists. And it is not irrelevant to my impromptu reflections, I think, to point out, in a conversational manner, a few things which I have had an opportunity to observe about it.

The first remark I would like to make is that the American approach to problems which will always trouble and harass mankind proceeds, it seems to me, from a desire to face things as they are courageously, and to discover a way of straightening them out, be it at the price of some more or less untoward simplification. In the case of young people (in whose eyes, for instance, the system of "going steady" enjoys the dignity of a kind of social institution) this approach appears to be less far-fetched, and more integrated in the publicly recognized rules and customs of social morality, than the European approach, but, let me say, more naive too, and, on occasion, more naively animal. The final result, as I see it, is not much better than that of the European approach, but not worse either, to be sure. Moreover, stating that the average sexual morals in this country are probably on a level with the average sexual morals in Europe is not to pay a particularly great compliment to either, or to human nature.

Yet it is in no way with the actual moral behavior of people that my few reflections are concerned; they have rather to do with their way of thinking. From this point of view it might be said that a growing preoccupation with sex is a quite general phenomenon in our contemporary Western world, but that in this country it takes particular forms—less depraved (by reason of basic American good will) than in certain sophisticated or literary European circles, and also sillier (by reason of the American confidence in facts and figures, statistics, "science," and the universal power of teaching). A quite peculiar sort of sex obsession, or, in more accurate terms, of studious, earnest and reverent concern for sex, is thus developing in the mental habits of the educated citizen: as if, once the yoke of Puritanism had been thrown off, American good will had discovered the realm of sex as a *terra incognita* of eminent and fascinating dignity, from whose conscientious exploration crucial discoveries in our own self-knowledge, and wonderful improvements in our human life should be expected.

Let us not speak of the foolish sexual sentimentalism of advertising lure and imagery. The most significant thing, to my mind, is the impact, on the new concern for sex I have mentioned, of the idea that everything, and especially human relations, is on the one hand matter for teaching and on the other hand matter for shallow rational explanation and so-called science—where all that counts is that which can be observed by the senses or by instruments, measured, and figured out.

Hence a general tendency to think of all great problems concerning human love in simple terms of sex; and a tendency, in many a cultivated person, to dismiss any idea of subjecting sexual life to supra-biological and supra-sociological ethical standards as a product either of religious prejudice or of a prudish or puritanical cast of mind. At the same time one can witness the development of a sort of religious reverence for the "facts of life" which is,

in my opinion, awfully stultifying. And instead of
the genuine sex education (integrated in a comprehensive knowledge of the whole human fabric) which
modern man needs very badly indeed, one can also
witness the preaching of a so-called sex education
in which cheap popularized science commingles
with soap-opera sentimentality and a most artlessly
serious-minded quest for the good. Competent doc-
tors, in a tepidly benevolent, cautious and paternal
style, uncover to attentive fathers and mothers of
families the mechanisms of sexual pleasure. And the
school system has classes in which respectable ma-
trons teach young ladies the best feminine techniques
through which male desires can be both stimulated
and kept under control, in order that these pupils,
naturally innocent and bookishly instructed, surprisingly bold and surprisingly calculating at the
same time, may catch and keep a boy and make a
happy marriage.

With respect to the common consciousness of the
country these things are more conspicuous than
really typical. The fact remains that it is a curious
spectacle to see so many people either teaching or
learning, through biology and psychology, how to be
happy in sexual life, plus a lot of items which, as a
rule, and since the beginning of things, nature has

had its own ready ways of making known to human beings free of Puritan or anti-Puritan complexes.

*

This chapter and the preceding one were not comprised in my original plan, because my main purpose was only to point out what I love in this country. Why did I include them?—For two reasons; first, by reason of you, dear reader,

Hypocrite lecteur, mon semblable, mon frère,
and of the mental habits of the public: if I did not speak of the disturbing aspects of the American scene—even assuming they were extraneous to my subject—I would appear to be concealing them on purpose, or be considered still more stupid and naive than I am.

The second reason is better: in reality the aspects in question are not extraneous to my subject. If we love a person or a country, it is only by looking at those things which carry into him or it the mark of the misery of human nature, and at the way in which he or it confronts them, that our own awareness of the reasons for our love is made complete. Only in the Kingdom of God has the devil no part. In the world, and in every nation of the world, he has his part. The question, for a given nation, is whether it likes or dislikes the fact, and whether it strives to turn evil to account or to get clear of it.

It is surely not for what I do not love in her that I love America. But in the very violence with which, far from trying to hide them, she lays bare her own evils, or the kind of avowal or open display she makes of them—and in the nerve and courage with which she struggles against them once she has become conscious of their malignancy—there is a deeply and genuinely human element which causes me to love her still more.

As regards the subject of the present chapter, and that silly infatuation with the idea of sex to which this country's misguided good will is now giving way, the American people are still in the first of the two stages of which I just spoke, the stage of open avowal. The second stage, the stage of effort and struggle toward recovery, is sure to come about. When psychologists and psychiatrists, who have a responsibility of their own for the infatuation in question, are made aware by statistics, and even perhaps a bit of common sense, of its destructive after-effects on the mental health of the nation, they will be among the first to crusade against it.

VIII

American Kindness and
Sense of Fellowship

When I think of American kindness, I remember not only the courtesy and generosity with which our American friends welcomed our small flock (my wife, her sister, and myself) in New York and tried to console us with their affection during the terrible months of the downfall of France, but also the sort of touching anonymous kindness which was shown us at every turn by unknown people at the same epoch: taxi drivers who said to us as we left the car, "Vive la France"; or the hawker who refused to let us pay for a bunch of flowers because we were French; or the Negro in charge of the elevator at the hotel who carefully concealed in his pocket the newspaper each time (that is, almost every day) the headlines announced a defeat of the French Army. These are small things, but when one is unhappy one is strangely comforted by such little things, which we never failed to meet in the streets of New York during that time.

*

Now I come to some more definite reflections.

The first remark I would like to submit is that there exists, in a general way, two opposite scales of values, in Europe and in this country.

The supreme value in the opinion of the European, especially the French, people, is, I think, *intelligence*—intelligence in contradistinction to goodness. If it is a question of the inner disposition of souls, I have no doubt that there is as much goodness in European people as in American people. There were, and there are, in Europe, saints who put divine love and love for the neighbor above all else. And if the French like to make a show of what is less good in them, it is in order to push the bad things outside, and thus to hide and shelter the good things inside which are their real treasure.

Yet I am speaking of a quite different thing: I am speaking of the accepted scale of values that people have in their minds and use in the conversation of ordinary life as well as in their external social behavior.

And I would say that in Europe, especially in France, "to be good" is synonymous with being naive, green, something of a simpleton. Wickedness, maliciousness—appears to be a condition required for intelligence. So it happens that when you return from this country to Europe, your first impression is that you are entering a wasp's nest. You are stung on all sides. (I remember a letter of an American residing in Paris, who wrote to a friend of his: "At last I am really accepted in the country, and treated like a Frenchman: today I was abused by my concierge, abused by a policeman, abused by the post office employees, and berated by two art critics.")

Now, there is some advantage in this cast of mind. It entails strong intellectual competition; the law of the survival of the fittest plays a not negligible part in European culture. And there is even some truth involved—for it is true that the intellectual virtues and the human virtues do not keep pace with one another. But the mistake consists in believing that everyone is an intellectual genius and has all the rights to maliciousness and aggressiveness involved.

If we turn now to the scale of values used in this country, it is just the opposite. The supreme value in the American scale of values is *goodness;* human reliability, good will, devotion, helpfulness. Hence, that American kindness which is so striking a feature to foreign visitors. Americans are ready to help, and happy to help. They are on equal terms of comradeship with everybody. And why? Simply because everybody is a human being. A fellow man. That's enough for him to be supposed worthy of assistance and sympathy—sometimes of exceedingly thoughtful and generous attention. When you arrive in this country you experience in this connection a strange, unforgettable sense of relief. You breathe more easily. And for all that, intelligence is not victimized.

*

I mentioned earlier the Manus of New Guinea. I would like to glance once again at this people who in twenty-five years jumped from the primitive to the civilized age, and at the impact that the passage of a million Americans through their island during the Second World War had on this anthropological phenomenon. Let us quote a few passages from the celebrated anthropologist Margaret Mead, in her book *New Lives for Old* [1]: "There is no reason to believe that the Americans, the some million Americans, who went through Manus represented in any way a specially selected, better mannered, or more idealistic section of the United States than any other such cross-section. Yet the Manus experienced them as a people whose relationships to each other were

1. New York: William Morrow. Copyright 1956 by Margaret Mead.

casteless and classless, where each man treated each other man as a human being." [1]

"The Americans treated us like individuals, like brothers," they said to the author.[2]

"The Americans believe in having work done by machines so that men can live to old age instead of dying worn out while they are still young." [3]

"As the Manus report it today, the Americans believed that every human being's life and health was of inestimable value, something for which no amount of property, time, and effort was too much to sacrifice . . . 'From the Americans we learned that human beings are irreplaceable and unexpendable, while all material things are replaceable and so expendable.' " [4]

" 'From the Americans we learned that it is *only* human beings that are important.' " [5]

Shall we conclude that Manus are more perspicacious than Europeans with their slogans about American materialism? Let us say, rather, that while remaining on their island, they had the unique opportunity of seeing Americans *at home*. The million Americans who passed through Manus were not there Americans abroad; they had America with

1. *Ibid.*, pp. 168–169.
2. *Ibid.*, p. 168.
3. *Ibid.*, p. 175.
4. *Ibid.*, p. 177.
5. *Ibid.*, p. 178.

them, that kind of roving American world which was the American army.

*

A particular result of the scale of values I mentioned above is that, as I said, we find here a general kindness, kindness to everyone, the extension of which is, so to speak, indefinite. But close friendship, with all the hardships and quarrels, and the human communion it involves, seems perhaps to have, as a result, a little less opportunity to develop. (Moreover, conversation must be pretty difficult if it is true that in this country, as a good lady said to my wife, "it is becoming to speak neither of the body, nor of the soul.") So it is that in the midst of general kindness and the busiest social life, it is not rare to find in individuals a feeling of loneliness: perhaps because there is a sort of opposition between openness to all and that close world which is the world of friendship.

That is a point I only submit. I don't know, but it seems to me that there is something there.

*

The last point I would like to make in this chapter is about mutual toleration and the sense of fellowship. This sense is tragically thwarted by prejudice when it comes to the race question. The fact remains,

however, that racial prejudice, as I previously remarked, is incompatible with the very tenets of the
American way of life and the deepest demands of the
American psyche, and that, as a result, this country
has set itself to eradicate it.

As to intellectual intolerance, intolerance with
respect to the philosophical or religious creeds of
co-citizens, it is no less destructive of the very tenets
of American life; and the American conscience has
triumphed over it. Speaking of New England culture
in the days of the Puritans, Paul Elmer More stated
that this culture passed through three successive
stages: religious intolerance, imaginative isolation,
nervous impotence. These are things of the past.
The danger inherent in the instincts of human
nature will always exist, to be sure. The Klan exists,
with its cross-burnings. Yet despite any tension, or
sporadic outburst of fear or anger, the American
public mind, as well as American law, has irrevocably
passed sentence on the use of violence, coercion,
slander, or menace against any dissenter. Mutual
toleration is an absolute necessity here, as a result
of the very fact that the American community is
made up of people from completely different national, social, and religious stocks. Without mutual
tolerance, everybody would be at each other's throat.

And that which was thus made obligatory by

historical necessity represents in itself, at the same time, an invaluable gain for civilization: people committed to live together in mutual respect and tolerance. America is the only country in the world where the vital importance of the sense of human fellowship is recognized in such a basic manner by the nation as a whole.

*

Let me add that even so great an achievement could sometimes be understood in the wrong way. Kindness is not all. As I put it a moment ago, intelligence is not victimized here by goodness and the sense of human fellowship. It might be, though. And in one particular case I think it is, namely in the case of high school education, where remarkably intelligent and devoted teachers seem to make kindness prevalent to such a point that the great thing is to have everybody equally happy and successful, and to train happy boys and girls in any talent of their own and any activity of social life—no matter how great the cost to genuine general culture and the fundamentals of integrated knowledge.

Coming now to more general considerations, I would like to observe that, as a result of a stronger community spirit, the conditions of intellectual life in this country differ somewhat from those in Europe. What I mean is that both organized intellectual effort and the general, collective intellectual work in the nation, the tilling of the soil for future intellectual harvests, and the general advance of research have much better possibilities here than in Europe. It is a fact that in more and more fields it has become imperative for scholars and the erudite in general as well as for scientists to acquaint themselves with what is going on in this country. But when it comes to the creative work of which a few are capable, and which demands solitary and ferocious obstinacy (and all the more dedication as nobody knows whether the result will be worth the pains), the conditions are, I would say, relatively less favorable: they involve a greater dislike for anything that entails a risk of separating the individual from the community.

I am thinking in particular of that kind of fear of outshining others which can sometimes be observed in academic circles. Many an American professor seems to be anxious not to be more brilliant or more original than the average member of the teaching community. After all, is not genius always harmful to mutual tolerance and a good state of affairs in the community, and is not mediocrity of good standing preferable to any occasion for jealousy, strife and rivalry?

Well, it is always enjoyable to have some fun at the expense of excessive reverence for community feelings. The fact remains that so far as intellectual life is concerned (this is the only perspective in which I am considering things at the present moment), the excessive reverence I just mentioned is peculiar to the academic world and even to its less remarkable elements. In more general terms let us say that between American intellectual life and European intellectual life there is a sort of dissymmetry, the one having often its weaker points with respect to qualities in which the other has its stronger ones, and conversely; but the one as a whole is at a level with the other as a whole. Moreover, American intellectual life, being in full growth, is at each moment able to develop unexpected potentialities. Today the emphasis is on science. In a few decades it may also be on the humanities or philosophy. In the realm of creative imagination, American novelists, poets, and critics are among those to whom modern literature owes its greatest achievements and most delicately penetrating investigations.

I do not forget, naturally, that field in which I have an interest of my own, the field of philosophy. Mortimer Adler was right in pointing out, in a recent article,[1] that the names of Charles Sanders

1. *San Francisco Chronicle,* February 4, 1957.

Peirce, Josiah Royce, William James, and John Dewey give clear proof of the fact that in the period of general growth which took place after the Civil War, American philosophers came to deserve the appreciation due to great intellectual personalities. Their work (which, whatever conflicting points of view and sharp oppositions it may involve, has in common, as I see it, a general concern for objectivity, and a thoughtful attention to every aspect of existence) shows how absurd is the notion, still accepted by many people who are ignorant of this country, that the American mind has a congenital aversion for abstract ideas, and for sustained and disinterested reflection.

This work, no doubt, still largely depends on the various intellectual currents which were born abroad, especially in Europe; it is nonetheless genuinely creative. For it causes a body of philosophical material of considerable extent to be tried, tested, revised and recast against the background of the American moral and cultural situation, and worked out into original doctrines.[1] So it is that now, as Herbert Schneider puts it,[2] a completely new chapter in American philosophy is being written by the pres-

1. Cf. Herbert Schneider, *A History of American Philosophy*, New York: Columbia Univ. Press, 1946; French trans., Paris: Gallimard, 1955.

2. *Ibid.*, French trans., Préface, p. 8.

ent generation. It is, I would add, no small achievement to have here a *Metaphysical Society* and a
Review of Metaphysics which have taken a stand
against all forms of positivism and against the concept that science is the only kind of valid knowledge
human reason is capable of. "That America has come
into its own philosophically seems undeniable,"
Mortimer Adler rightly stated. "Where we fall short,
as compared with the older philosophical countries
of Europe, is in public interest and participation
and in further penetration of philosophy into the
intellectual and political life of the nation. But this
too will doubtless come in time."

*

For the time being there is indeed in American
ways—I would like to mention it parenthetically—a
particular point which offers little cause for elation,
namely the attitude of public opinion toward intellectuals, especially toward artists. In France artists
are kings; everybody is interested in their doings
and in the opinion of a great novelist or a great
painter on national affairs. Here, on the contrary,
their opinions carry less weight than that of prom-
inent businessmen; furthermore, and this is more
serious, they seem to arouse some suspicion, and
communion between the beholder and the artist is

lacking in the very place where it should exist, namely, in that area which, though indeed larger than the small group of expert connoisseurs, is narrower than the general public, and which may be called the enlightened public. As to the connoisseurs, their fondness for art and their taste are especially remarkable here (one has only to think of the incomparable treasures in modern painting which have been brought to this country by the intelligent choice of private collectors). The general public has as vulgar a taste here as everywhere, though there is in them an eagerness to understand which could produce astonishing results if it were cultivated. But what about the enlightened public, with which I am particularly concerned? What the enlightened public expects from the artist is, doubtless, some kind of genuine intellectual enjoyment, and in general they are pretty good judges. But I am afraid they are no more interested in the inner creative effort of a painter or a writer than, I would say, in that of the cook who prepares food for them in restaurants. They enjoy the work as they enjoy the food, but the quest and discoveries of the artist in the proper field of art and poetry, his creative agony, stirs almost no one, I believe, outside the closed world of the artists and connoisseurs themselves.

77

*

To close this parenthesis, and come back to my subject, there is, I would observe, a possible mistake on the requirements of mutual toleration which, in my opinion, it is important to be aware of.

One happens sometimes to meet people who think that a primary condition of tolerance and peaceful co-existence is not to believe in any truth or not to adhere firmly to any assertion as unshakeably true in itself. May I say that these people are, in fact, the most intolerant people, for if perchance they were to believe in something as unshakeably true, they would feel compelled by the same stroke to impose by force and coercion their own belief on their fellow men. The only remedy they have found for their abiding tendency to fanaticism is to cut themselves off from truth. As a result, they insist that whoever knows or claims to know truth or justice simply cannot be a good citizen "because he cannot and is not expected to admit the possibility of a view different from his own, the *true* view."

Well, if it were true that whoever knows or claims to know truth or justice cannot admit the possibility of a view different from his own, and is bound to impose his true view on other people by violence, the rational animal would be the most dangerous of beasts. In reality, it is through rational means, that is, through persuasion, not coercion, that man is bound by his very nature to try to induce others to share in what he knows or claims to know as true and just. Be it a question of science, metaphysics, or religion, the man who says "What is truth?", as Pilate did, is not a tolerant man, but a betrayer of the human race. There is, in other words, real and genuine tolerance only when a man is firmly and absolutely convinced of a truth, or of what he holds to be a truth, and when, at the same time, he recognizes the right of those who deny this truth to exist, and to contradict him, and to speak their own mind, not because they are free from truth but because they seek truth in their own way, and because he respects in them human nature and human dignity, and those very resources and living springs of the intellect and of conscience which make them potentially capable of attaining the truth he loves, if some day they happen to see it.

The views I have just criticized about the "what is truth?" supposedly required by mutual toleration are not specifically American—it was Kelsen who made a system of them. Moreover, when you hear them expressed—not infrequently, I would say—in this country, they are much more an easy-going way of speaking than an expression of serious views to

GARY LIBRARY
VERMONT   COLLEGE

be put into practice. In actual fact what people think is rather that a kind of humility always keeps pace with the spirit of tolerance. And this is perfectly true.

I don't believe, nevertheless, that it is without utility explicitly to realize that doubt and intellectual timidity are not a prerequisite for mutual toleration; and that it is truth, not ignorance, which makes us humble, and gives us the sense of what remains unknown in our very knowledge. In one sense there is wisdom in appealing to our ignorance, if we mean the ignorance of those who know, not the ignorance of those who are in the dark.

II

IX

"We Are Bruised Souls"

I would like to put the next three chapters within a single framework. They have to do with things which, under the visible signs that point to them, have a secret, spiritual meaning, and which refer to the presence—unconscious and undeliberate, and too ordinary, too daily to be noticed as a rule—of a certain hidden disposition that is Christian in origin, and appears to me as a kind of humble and remote reminiscence of the Gospel in the inner attitude of people. Behind the façade of violence and callousness of modern life, this something of old, subtle Christian flavor lies, I think, deep in the soul of this country.

My first reflections in this regard may be grouped under the heading, *"We are bruised souls."*

These words were said to me many years ago by a great American for whom I have profound respect and affection. They struck me in an indelible manner. They alluded to the wounds and sorrows of ancestors, and that memory of the sufferings caused by persecution and prejudice which they left to their progeny as a spiritual patrimony; they related to the fact that the ancestors of today's Americans were people hunted because of their religious convictions, rejected by their national community, or offended and humiliated by distress and poverty.

At this point we may grasp the hidden meaning of the basic part played by immigration in the life of this country. Each day, each year brings to the shores of America a flux of men and women who come from every part of the world and every cultural tradition, nearly broken by the moral persecutions, moral distress or physical poverty suffered in the Old World.

They come over to commit all their remaining forces to the common task of the land of promise which receives them. Their children will be told of their sufferings and keep them in memory, but they will share in the youthful force, hope, and activity of their new national community. They will embark on the pursuit of happiness.

With respect to this basic sociological datum: the perpetual arrival of a new first generation of immigrants, as well as to the arrival of the first colonists, one might say that the tears and sufferings of many unfortunates have been and ceaselessly are a stream fecundating the soil of the New World and preparing for America's grandeur.

The extraordinary fact is that these tears are not shed *in vain,* I mean with regard to the earthly destiny of the children of man. Here lies, in my opinion, a distinctive privilege of this country, and a deep human mystery concealed behind its power and prosperity. The tears and sufferings of the persecuted and unfortunate are transmuted into a perpetual effort to improve human destiny and to make life bearable; they are transfigured into optimism and creativity.

But what is the objective meaning of that transmutation of the sufferings of the poor and the wounded into a new strength and a new hope—if not a Christian meaning projected into the sphere of temporal, social and political existence? Except under the shade of the Gospel such a phenomenon could neither take place nor make sense in human history.

*

The sentence I am commenting upon here, *"We are bruised souls,"* bears witness to a kind of bruise or wound which is, I would say, of an evangelical nature: because wounds which cause a human soul to be compassionate are evangelical wounds; and such a sentence offers us, I think, the deepest reason for the sense of mercy and pity, and the sense of responsibility toward all those in distress, which are rooted in the collective American psyche, deep beneath the hardness and harshness of the hunt for material interests and advantages which is the object of ordinary activity and ordinary conversation. This spark of the Gospel lying deep in people who more often than not do not think at all of the Gospel, is not a thing that one speaks of. It is hidden in the secret life of souls, and covered by all the ordinary selfish desires and concerns of human nature. It exists, however, and is active in the great mass of the nation. And what is more valuable in this poor world than to find a trace of Gospel fraternal love active among men?

There is, in the most existential sense, a strain of Gospel fraternal love deep in the American blood.

*

I spoke a moment ago of the spiritual importance of immigration for this country. Probably immigration will pose more difficult problems in proportion as the country becomes more populated. It is to be hoped that that strange source of insuperable strength and energy which comes from the influx of the poor and the humiliated, welcomed here to live a worthy human life, will never cease to vitalize American civilization. Without this humble source, namely the tears and sufferings of the poor pouring into the flux of American life and transmuted into human energy, America would lose an essential ingredient of her spiritual identity.

Finally, in the light of the considerations I have submitted, we may understand why this nation, which is principally a middle-class nation, nevertheless is not a "bourgeois" nation. There is another basic reason for this fact, which is sociological. I shall touch upon it later.[1] The reason of which I am now speaking refers to the spiritual aspect of the question, the old bruise in the soul.

Thus, let me say, you have gangsters, racketeers, crooked lawyers, gamblers, small home-owners who grow conservative and thirsty for security as they grow richer; you have social climbers, cheap politicians, hard-boiled businessmen, metallic women, well-to-do people of fashion—you have no Bourgeois. That is one of the blessings of this country.

1. See *infra,* chapter XIX, pp. 175–178.

X

The Symbolic Smile

There is a saying of St. Teresa of Avila which seems to me particularly significant. She used to say, "Without poetry life would not be tolerable."

I think that behind all the improvements in the material conditions of existence which are to be seen in this country, there is a great, steady effort to *make life tolerable.*

Let me note, in passing, that the effort in question does not presuppose a particularly optimistic view of *things as they are;* since things as they are must be changed.

Well, coming back to my own line of reflection, I would say that the accusation of materialism, technocratic inhumanity, etc., appears especially unfair in this light. Of course, here as elsewhere in the world, industrial civilization entails the temptation of materialist technocratism. But this country, which seems at first glance more threatened by such a temptation because it is more industrialized, has, in reality, a better chance of overcoming it, because from the very start the American effort is directed toward the good of man, the humble dignity of man in each one of us.

It is too easy for certain high-brow Europeans with large bank accounts and delicious wine in their cellars to make fun of all gadgets—bathtubs, refrigerators, dishwashers, washing machines, kitchen appliances, vacuum cleaners and so on, which everybody, so to speak—that is, a very great number of people of slender resources, the majority of the nation—enjoy here. (The same European critics hasten, incidentally, to buy the gadgets in question as soon as they can.) These gadgets serve, in actual fact, to make material life less overwhelming for common humanity, and to emancipate the human being from the servitude of matter in the midst of the chores of everyday life. Further: improvements in housing create better moral conditions for man and family life. And, in general, those improvements which concern the great mass of the people are of a nature to restore within human beings a sense of inner freedom at the most elementary level.

For instance, a woman here can be elegantly dressed in low-priced attire. Now everybody knows how important (not only esthetically but also ethically) it is for a woman not to feel humiliated by her clothes.

*

The yearning to make life tolerable is best revealed, it seems to me, in the American smile.

You meet on American streets smiling faces, which plunge you into a stream of quite general and anonymous good feeling. Of course, there is an immense part of illusion, of ritually accepted illusion, in the universal benignancy thus displayed. I had a dentist in a small town whose nurses were so well trained that you were dazzled by their radiant smiles and their unshakeable optimism. Finally you came to think, in a kind of daydream, that the fact of dying in the midst of these happy smiles and the angel wings of these white, immaculate uniforms, would be a pure pleasure, a moment of no consequence. Relax, take it easy, it's nothing. Thereafter, you would enjoy the cleanness and happiness of the funeral home, and the chattering of your friends around your embalmed corpse. . . .

I left this dentist, in order to protect within my mind the Christian idea of death.

*

Yet I have another recollection. I remember I was in Washington on a day in 1940, when the first news arrived of the invasion of France by the Germans. I was in utter loneliness, with personal problems and anxieties that weighed heavily on me. In this frame of mind I went to a small restaurant to have lunch, and was served by a waitress who displayed for me a sweet anonymous American smile. I knew perfectly well that it was mere illusion, as unreal a thing as "the smile of an absent cat." And nevertheless I felt comforted by this mirage, all the more comforted as I knew I had absolutely nothing to expect from these merely symbolic good feelings, and therefore no possibility of being disappointed.

And I suddenly realized the meaning of this symbol, the general, elementary, deep-seated sense of common human pilgrimage and brotherhood which exists in this country and lies behind the smile in question. After all, to feel disheartened and forsaken was only an episode. I am grateful to this waitress for having helped me one day against hopelessness.

Deep beneath the anonymous American smile there is a feeling that is evangelical in origin—compassion for man, a desire to make life tolerable. This symbolic smile is a kind of anonymous reply of the human soul, which refuses to acknowledge itself vanquished by the pressure of the assembly line, or the big anonymous machinery of modern civilization.

XI

The American Pilgrimage

We are confronted in this country with a curious paradoxical contrast. Nobody seems less indifferent to the world and to the goods of this world, more eager to work on it, to transform it (not so much in order to enjoy it, but in order to make it better) than the American people. But at the same time one feels in them a kind of strange, insuperable detachment.

Americans seem to be in their own land as pilgrims, prodded by a dream. They are always on the move—available for new tasks, prepared for the possible loss of what they have. They are not *settled*, *installed* (I would say in French, *"installés"*—a word which carries a strong moral connotation) though a trend toward an ideal of security has been developing since the war. Yet they are still far from being a *settled* people.

I find a symbol of the spiritual disposition I am mentioning in those small wooden houses with which this country is strewn. They are like cabins, which in a few years will fade away. Looking at them, one is reminded of St. Paul's saying: "As in a land not his own, dwelling in tents."

As you know, Rockefeller Center was built on a plot leased for ninety-nine years. A sky-scraper in New York does not lay claim to brave the centuries any more than does a tent in the desert. Let us think, by way of contrast, of the Pyramids of pagan Egypt, and the pride of the Pharaohs!

And now Americans are demolishing houses and constructing new buildings all over New York. New York is in the moult once again.

This sense of becoming, this sense of the flux of time and the dominion of time over everything here below, can be interpreted, of course, in merely pragmatist terms. It can turn into the worship of becoming and change. It can develop a cast of mind which, in the intellectual field, would mean a horror of any tradition, the denial of any lasting and supra-temporal value. But such a cast of mind is but a degeneration of the inner mood of which I am speaking. In its genuine significance this American mood seems to me to be close to Christian detachment, to the Christian sense of the impermanence of earthly things. Those now with us must fade away if better ones are to appear.

In this sense of becoming and impermanence one may discern a feeling of evangelical origin which has been projected into temporal activity.

XII

American Modesty

The popular image of the Yankee boasting that he has the biggest car or runs the biggest business in the world is, in my opinion, utterly misleading. My experience with American students taught me quite another thing. I was struck by their modesty—even, sometimes, surprised at the slight value they seemed to attach to their own personal opinion as long as they had not examined the various views of all the experts in the matter.

My experience with many of my colleagues led me to the same conclusion. One of my most distinguished students at the Graduate School at Princeton was a Jesuit Father; and the members of the department seemed to be, at the beginning, as intimidated by him as he was by them. That was the first time, I assume, that a Jesuit Father had got his doctorate in philosophy at Princeton with a (quite remarkable) dissertation on Thomas Aquinas. But mutual esteem and appreciation grew rapidly between him and them, and a professor, who is a good friend of mine, said to me one day: "I like your Jesuit Father very much. I enjoy my talks with him. His way of think-ing is really American; he doesn't have all the an-swers; he is able to say, 'I don't know.' . . ."

Finally I came to realize that this distrust of self-assertion and self-reliance was a general feature of the American mind. Of course I know there are still some people in this country who pass judgment on European nations with all the more contempt and severity as they know nothing or almost nothing about them. If my present reflections are true, we should say that in doing so these people (they are fewer and fewer, I hope) show an un-American men-tal attitude. In actual fact there is an American *mod-esty* before life and reality which is a great moral virtue and a dynamic quality of considerable efficacy.

It originates, I think, in a sense of the complexity of things; of the fluidity of life which escapes our concepts; and of the multiple aspects of reality which make our judgments precarious. Hence, a circum-spection before taking a stand or reaching a con-clusion; a passion for blueprints; a slowness (which is an exasperating surprise for European visitors) in preparatory processes, and an extreme boldness and rapidity in execution; an extraordinary power of unceasing change, renewal, and adaptation to the growth of history.

*

This modesty is essentially linked with what might be called the *experiential approach,* in which it is necessary to get all factual data, all points of view and all possible opinions before making a judgment— itself tentative.

Now, let me say, a single idea, if it is right, saves us the labor of an infinity of experiences. (That is why a Frenchman starts with his own idea.) Yes, but the idea must be right. If it is wrong, it involves us in infinite trouble. Thus it is that a sound distrust of ideology seems quite advisable in practical matters, especially if we remember that the discovery of new true ideas is, as a rule, prodded on by some alluring folly which preys upon them.

In this country the general distrust of ideology proceeds from the modesty before reality to be grasped—and to be improved—the eager modesty of which I am speaking, rather than from sheer empiricism.

Yet—and here is the dark side of the picture—it is liable to veer toward empiricism, and to a general and systematic Fear of ideas. If this cast of mind— Fear of ideas, and of intellectual intuition—became prevalent, it would involve the danger of impairing intellectual creativity; the risk, for instance, of making, not new applications, but new fundamental discoveries, much more difficult in the field of science.

There would be a risk, also, of imperiling the deep-rooted intellectual convictions, rationally founded, which man needs for the conduct of his life.

In particular, the moral tenets of a free people—justice; freedom; equality; human rights—would risk becoming a matter of feeling and national tradition, or adjustment to the environment, instead of being held as objective values, justifiable in reason.

Then, on the one hand, these moral tenets would lose their inner vigor in each individual. They would become more or less relativized, subjectivized. And on the other hand, they would lose their intelligible universality, and communicability, their impact on the minds of other peoples, that persuasive, illuminating, *apostolic* power which is peculiar to ideas.

Here I come to a point which is, to my mind, of especial interest, namely the need, with respect to genuine human communication, for a proper ideology—better to say, a proper intellectual expression—or an explicit philosophy and an explicitly formulated ideal.

It is through ideas that we communicate with other minds. It is through ideas that anything we have achieved or discovered in concrete life is made known to others, and even to ourselves.

Now the distrust of ideas, the too great ideological modesty of which I am speaking,[1] involves a serious risk: the risk of intellectual isolation, the risk of making American reality, and the greatest human and social achievements of the American people, noncommunicable to other nations, and walled up in themselves, as long as ideology or philosophy remains far behind real and actual behavior.

1. This modesty is partly responsible, it seems to me, for another kind of harm: I mean the spreading of the notion (imported from Germany) that only specialists have a right to think—and that each one of them, moreover, is all the more competent in his own field, and all the more reliable, as he shuns knowing anything outside the field in question.

XIII

Too Much Modesty
The Need for an Explicit Philosophy

I would like to submit an especially significant example of the need for an explicit philosophy, an example drawn from the achievements and discoveries of this country in the social field. I am thinking of a phenomenon of great historical importance —the striking success of the "unsystematic American system": namely, the transformation of the economic system which has come about in this country during the last half century.

The industrial regime inherited from Europe has now become unrecognizable in this country. It has been superseded by new economic structures which are still in the making, and in a state of fluidity, but which render both capitalism and socialism things of the past.

Free enterprise and private ownership function now in a social context and a general mood entirely different from those of the nineteenth century.

Two developments of outstanding significance must be mentioned in this connection: first, the growth of organized labor; second, the evolution of industry and management.

*

Let us first say a few words on the growth of organized labor.

A hundred years ago, and still at the dawn of this century, the situation of workers was no better in America than in Europe in the dark days of the Industrial Revolution. It paralleled the description of the wretched life of the proletariat given by Marx. Most of the pioneers of unionization, obscure forgotten forerunners destined to be sacrificed, were hopelessly broken, sometimes by their own fellow workers.

The bitter fights in which violence of all kinds was used to crush the beginnings of labor organization, and in which victory could be obtained only by dint of dedicated courage—and ruthlessness—were still raging in the first decades of the twentieth century (it was in 1903, in the course of a long and finally victorious strike of anthracite coal miners, that George F. Baer wrote his famous "divine right" letter; [1] it was in 1914 that the Ludlow Massacre took place).[2]

1. In this letter George F. Baer, president of the Philadelphia and Reading Company, wrote: "The right and interests of the laboring man will be protected and cared for—not by the labor agitators, but

The progress in social legislation, which reached its acme with the passage of the National Labor Relations Act in 1935, and granted labor rights of fundamental import, played—as did the unbending effort of labor itself and of its stiff-necked leaders—an essential part in the process of transformation.

And now—now the average standard of living of the American worker is the highest in the world, and makes possible for the majority of them a decent human life. Organized labor has become such a formidable power (with huge financial means which enables it to have its own institutions of social welfare, hospitals, media of mass communication), that it confronts big corporations as an equal, and is sure it can oblige them to come to terms. The policy of its high command, moreover, is to try to get the best

---

by the Christian men to whom God in His infinite wisdom has given the control of the property interests of the country, and upon the successful management of which so much depends." Cf. Saul Alinsky, *John L. Lewis, An Unauthorized Biography,* New York: 1949, Putnam, p. 12.

The strike was finally victorious thanks to the strong intervention of President Theodore Roosevelt, which obliged the mine owners to capitulate.

2. In the course of a strike the management of the mines of Ludlow, Colorado, "fought the union in every conceivable way, importing the Baldwin-Felts Detective Agency, which rode around in an armored car shooting down strikers on sight. They got injunctions and indictments against labor organizers. They evicted miners and their families from company homes into the freezing temperatures of a Colorado winter. To meet this forced exodus, the union set up tents, where soon hundreds of miners and their families were sheltered.

"The tension increased, and the militia was called in under the

possible conditions without putting the progress of production in jeopardy; for, as a result of the growing commitments themselves of organized labor, and of the fact that its resources come from portions automatically withheld from the wages of its members, it appears that the very power of labor needs great

---

command of a Major Patrick Hamrock. Early on the morning of April 20, 1914, just as this tent community was preparing for breakfast, the state militia attacked. *The New York Times* (April 21, 1914) reported: 'The Ludlow Camp is a mass of charred debris and buried beneath a story of horror unparalleled in the history of industrial warfare. In holes that had been dug for their protection against the rifle fire, the women and children died like rats when the flames swept over them. One pit uncovered this afternoon disclosed the bodies of ten children and two women.' " *Ibid.*, pp. 9–10.

In the background of the American labor movement there was no lack of other human victims, like "the Haymarket martyrs who had been 'framed' and put to death in Chicago in 1887" (Cf. Dorothy Day, *The Long Loneliness*, New York: 1952, Harper, p. 46), or the men, women and children trampled down by mounted police in the Tompkins Square riot in New York (January 13, 1874), or that Joe Hill who was unjustly condemned and shot to death in Salt Lake City, in 1915, and whose ashes in tiny envelopes were scattered to the winds by his friends all over the country, and abroad—a migratory worker who had composed most of the songs of the I.W.W., and who became himself the hero of a ballad. On Joe Hill (Joseph Hillstrom) see Ralph Chaplin, *Wobbly*, The University of Chicago Press, 1948, chapter XVI. I am grateful to Professor Willard Thorp of Princeton University for bringing this book to my attention.

On the Haymarket Square riot in 1886 see Foster Rhea Dulles, *Labor in America*, New York: Thomas Y. Crowell Co., 1949, 1955, pp. 122–125. On the Homestead and Pullman strikes (1892 and 1894), see *ibid.*, chapter X. The author points out that in the combat against labor organization certain operators did not hesitate to use not only strikebreakers but also *agents provocateurs* (even from among the "Molly Maguires," *ibid.*, p. 117), and dynamite planting (*ibid.*, p. 216).

industry as the very prosperity of great industry needs labor. American labor has of course its own internal tensions and conflicts; it must bring to completion rather difficult cleaning-up operations in a few unions; it is exposed to the ordinary risks of bigness and institutionalization. For all that, we may believe that its ever-growing power, as well as the sense of responsibility, and the interest in the general problems of civilization it is developing, will make it, in a not too distant future, one of the most decisive forces in the history of the nation, and of mankind.

*

I come now to the evolution of industry and management, which is, in one sense, more surprising than the rapid and successful ascension of American labor, for it has to do with a transformation in the capitalist structure itself. It is, too, a typically American phenomenon. The striking fact in this regard is that the corporations,[1] while growing, have, at the same time, undergone deep inner changes; so that a journalist could write apropos of a conference organized in 1951 by the Corning Glass Works: "When I was growing up, 'soulless corporation' was a very common term . . . Well, in my lifetime I have seen

1. On the nature of the American corporation, see Peter F. Drucker, *Concept of the Corporation,* New York: Day, 1946; and *The Practice of Management,* New York: Harper, 1954.

a remarkable change in this. I don't know whether it could be said that corporations have obtained a soul, but at least they have obtained intelligence." [1] These big organisms, collectively-structured and managed, are still fondly thinking, to be sure, of the dividends of their stockholders [2]—but not as the unique, even

1. Ralph Coghlan, in the St. Louis *Post Dispatch*. Quoted by Frederick Lewis Allen, *The Big Change*, New York, Harper, 1952, p. 252.

"So it seems," Adolf Berle writes, "the corporations have a conscience, or else accept direction from the conscience of the government. This conscience must be built into institutions so that it can be invoked as a right by the individuals and interests subject to the corporate power." Adolf A. Berle, *The 20th Century Capitalist Revolution*, New York: Harcourt Brace, 1954, pp. 113–114.

2. Stockholders tend more and more to become mere profit-sharers with no control over the management of the enterprise. *Cf.* Peter Drucker, *The New Society*, New York: Harper, 1949, p. 340: "There is absolutely nothing in the nature of investment that either requires or justifies ownership rights, that is, rights of control. A future age may well regard the idea that control of a productive organization of human beings can be bought and sold for money, in the same light in which we today regard the buying and selling of human beings under slavery."

Even the right of stockholders to the profits made by corporations is subject to limitation: "Twenty-nine states have already passed statutes authorizing corporations, both presently existing and subsequently organized, to make contributions to philanthropy and education. Constitutional validity of one of these statutes—that of New Jersey—was the subject of a recent test case (A. P. Smith Manufacturing Company v. Ruth Barlow, *et al.*) and was forthrightly upheld by the New Jersey Supreme Court. The Supreme Court of the United States dismissed appeal, holding that no Federal question was involved. For practical purposes, the state has authorized corporations to withhold from their shareholders a portion of their profits, channeling it to schools, colleges, hospitals, research, and other good causes." Adolf Berle, *op. cit.*, pp. 168–169.

as the first thing; because they have understood that, in order simply to exist, and to keep producing, they must become more and more socially minded and concerned with the general welfare. Thus, not by reason of any Christian love, but rather of intelligent self-interest, and of the ontological generosity, so to speak, of the stream of life, the idea of the advantage of the human being—all those who cooperate on the job,[1] and the general public as well—is gradually taking the upper hand. I do not assume that corporations have reached a stage where they would prefer the common good to their own particular good. But they are reaching a stage where for the sake of their own particular good they realize that the superior rights of the common good must be taken into account.

"The Tycoon is dead"—or dying—as the editors of *Fortune* magazine put it in an advertisement for their book, *U.S.A.—The Permanent Revolution*. And as a result, corporations tend to become kinds of autonomous communities, in which one-man management is supplanted by team management, and which involve such inner complexity and differentia-

1. Paradoxically enough (this is a remark of Saul Alinsky's) one of the industries in which this concern—sometimes too pervasive indeed—for the human welfare of the individuals involved is most developed, is the one whose products are intended to make the human brain superfluous—the International Business Machines Corporation.

tion that a new function is now developing in them—
the function of instructors in human relations, who
teach applied psychology to the various branches of
a given industry, and who foster human understanding between them.[1]

There is a great deal of planning, both spontane-

1. An especially interesting document, in this connection, is the
"Fundamentals in Management, a Basic Guide for Executive Development" prepared by John Hite, Director of Training, Johnson and
Johnson, for the Institutes in Leadership and Management for Manufacturing, Research and Sales personnel throughout the corporation.

See also *Human Relations in Modern Business*, A Guide for Action
sponsored by American Business Leaders. Copyright 1949 by Prentice-
Hall, Inc., Englewood Cliffs, N.J. I quote some lines (pp. 14–15) from
this booklet, in which General Robert Wood Johnson had a not
small part:

"Employees do offer their services in a competitive or a regulated
market. But these same employees are men. They have human hearts
and minds. They love and they are loved. They have their moments
of noble desire, and their lapses into evil ways. They are average
men with average lives.

"Most of them do not ask much from the world, but their basic
needs are vital to them. Their first demand upon society is that they
be treated as human beings, not as machines.

". . . Men want self-respect, the respect of others, a chance to
live, some assurance of security, and a social life. If we concentrate
upon only one of these needs and neglect the others, men become
unhappy and frustrated. This was the fallacy behind the notion of
the 'economic man.' It dealt only with the desire for survival. It
assumed that if employees received sufficient wages so that they were
fed, clothed, and housed adequately, they would be content. But
such a limited approach is bad psychology and bad ethics. It ignores
vital needs and noble aims of man's nature. It fails to respect his
inner dignity, based on his spiritual nature, his origin from God,
and his destiny in God's plan for the universe. Even though men
may or may not be fully conscious of these noble sanctions, they must
be taken into account." Reprinted by permission of the publisher.

ous (thanks to the staff of economists employed by each big corporation) and connected and intermingled with State and Federal legislation, and government regulations and proddings.

The old merciless struggles between management and labor, during the heroic period of labor organization, have given way to a new relationship in which the antagonisms are still basically serious, but in the last analysis are reduced to a kind of cooperative tension, with enormous social advances such as the annual wage guaranteed to workers by some big industries, and contracts tying wages to productivity. A number of companies have introduced profit-sharing. And it would not be surprising, I think, if one day, contrary to now prevailing opinions, the American creative imagination were to find an unforeseen way of having labor share in the management as well. In any case it may be said that one of the changes the next generation will witness here will be a change in the very role and function of the union: this role and function becoming more deeply and organically basic in the whole economic process, and the union evolving from a merely antagonistic force (in accordance with the pattern employment-versus-labor which was peculiar to the capitalistic economy of old) into a necessary and responsible counter-balancing power, "a less emotionally divisive though equally effective part of the organizational machinery of American business." [1]

Finally, one of the most striking characteristics of the picture is the infinite swarming, on the American scene, of private groups, study clubs, associations, committees, which are designed "to look out for one aspect or another of the common good," and whose activity is interlocked in an inextricable manner with that of government agencies, other private groups, universities, business and industry. The effect is a spontaneous and steady collective regulation and prodding of the tremendous effort of the whole country, which is of invaluable importance.

All this is only a beginning in an immense and difficult task—the humanization of the industrial regime. The social advances I have mentioned entail in the case of large corporations the usual drawbacks of gigantism, not to speak of the "promotion neurosis" which threatens executives.[2] The power of big money is still big itself, very big indeed. And the tremendous power of corporations and corporate management, in proportion as it grows, must, as a matter of public interest, be lawfully counterbalanced and regulated by various other powers. Serious problems

1. F. L. Allen, *op. cit.,* p. 237.
2. Cf. *The Executive Life,* by the Editors of *Fortune,* New York: Doubleday, 1956.

are posed by the deeper and deeper alliance of great corporations with government, and by the fact that their gradual awakening to their obligations toward the general welfare—and, in the last analysis, toward the political common good of the nation—means that in actual existence they willy-nilly play a specifically political role [1] in democratic society. Though I trust that these problems will be satisfactorily solved —as well as those which relate to the political role which organized labor is, inevitably, also called to play in the future—this will nevertheless require much time, much human energy and dedicated effort. The struggle between the spirit of the people and the logic of the industrial system will go on in new forms and in new phases, while the industrial system

1. This point, to which I only allude in passing, is discussed on its own merits in Adolf Berle's and Scott Buchanan's books mentioned on p. 117. Adolf Berle concludes: "Corporate managements, like others, knowingly or unknowingly, are constrained to work within a frame of surrounding conceptions which in time impose themselves. The price of failure to understand and observe them is decay of the corporation itself. Such conceptions emerge in time as law. It may be said of the corporation as old Bracton said of the Crown: 'There is no king where the will and not the law prevails.'" *The 20th Century Capitalist Revolution*, p. 188.

Scott Buchanan writes, in a similar vein: "As Plutarch in the life of Crassus says, when economy deals with men as well as things there is polity. It would seem that a full recognition of this in principle should lead to a full study and revision of our visible and invisible governments, and that this study might play midwife at the birth of a new political liberty." *Essay in Politics*, New York: Philosophical Library, 1953, p. 192.

itself will be led by scientific progress to new technical revolutions. The gradual realization of the American ideal of equal opportunity for all, and progress in social justice, will be the work of generations. But the road is open, the guiding spirit on which the whole ritual of economy finally depends has changed; a rupture with the old forms of the industrial regime has taken place.

*

In order to confirm the too hasty and imperfect outline I just made, permit me to quote some passages from the last chapter of Frederick Lewis Allen's book, *The Big Change,* which I have already mentioned. This chapter appeared first in *Harper's Magazine,* June, 1952.

"For the March 4, 1951 issue of *This Week,* . . . the editor, William I. Nichols, wrote an article called: 'Wanted: A New Name for Capitalism.' Arguing that the word is no longer the right one to fit our present American system, because in too many people's minds, especially in other parts of the world, 'it stands for the primitive economic system of the nineteenth century,' Mr. Nichols asked: 'How shall we describe this system—imperfect, but always improving, and always capable of further improvement —where men move forward together, working together, building together, producing always more and more, and sharing together the rewards of their increased production?' He said he had heard various suggestions, such as 'the new capitalism,' 'democratic capitalism,' 'economic democracy,' 'industrial democracy,' 'distributism,' 'mutualism,' and 'productivism,' but wondered if there might not be a better term. And he invited readers to write in their own suggestions in a coupon printed in the magazine.

"Fifteen thousand coupons came back with suggestions. 'Never in my whole editorial experience,' said Mr. Nichols afterward, 'have I touched so live a nerve.' " [1]

Mr. Allen himself seems to prefer the word "managementism." I would suggest that the expression "economic humanism" would probably be more pleasing to the ear, and more accurate.

Well, by virtue of the mechanics of the capitalist system, as it was received from Europe, the author observes that "at the turn of the century America seemed in danger of becoming a land in which the millionaires had more and more and the rest had less and less, and where a few financiers had a strangle hold, not only on the country's economic apparatus, but on its political apparatus too." "This," he goes on to say, and I attach particular importance to the remark, "this outraged the democratic spirit of the

1. F. L. Allen, "The Unsystematic American System," *Harper's Magazine*, June, 1952, p. 21.

country, the national sense of fair play. So we went to work to change things—not by revolution but by a series of experimental revisions of the system. The reform movement in the early years of this century—that revolt of the American conscience which was kindled by Theodore Roosevelt, the elder La Follette, and Woodrow Wilson," resulted in the fact that "through a combination of patchwork revisions of the system—tax laws, minimum wage laws, subsidies and guarantees and regulations of various sorts, plus labor union pressures and new management attitudes—we had repealed the Iron Law of Wages. We had brought about an automatic redistribution of income from the well-to-do to the less well-to-do . . . We had discovered a new frontier to open up: the purchasing power of the poor.

"That, it seems to me, is the essence of the Great American Discovery. And it has its corollary: that if you thus bring advantages to a great lot of previously underprivileged people, they will rise to their opportunities and, by and large, will become responsible citizens." [1]

Thus it is that a new social and economic regime is, in actual fact, developing in this country—a phenomenon which gives the lie to the forecasts of Karl Marx, and which came about not by virtue of some

1. *Ibid.*, p. 22.

kind of inner necessity in the evolution of capitalism which Marx had overlooked, but by virtue of the freedom and spirit of man, namely by virtue of the American mind and conscience, and of the American collective effort of imagination and creation.

Philosophically speaking, I would say that individual profit still remains, as it ever will, an indispensable human incentive, but that it is now definitely losing absolute primacy; and that the principle of the fecundity of money is definitely superseded now by the principle of profit-sharing in a contractual association.

This new social and economic regime is still in a state of full becoming, but it has already brought human history beyond both capitalism and socialism. As the same author puts it, "The United States is not evolving toward socialism, but past socialism . . . It is time we realized that when we battle against communism, we are battling against the past, not against the future." [1]

Here we have a decisive fact in modern history; and this fact is a considerable success of the experiential approach dear to the American mind.

*

Yes. But now I return to my point, namely to the

1. *Ibid.,* p. 25.

need for an adequate ideology, or philosophy. And I ask: who in the world is aware of this decisive fact which we have just discussed?

Even in this country, as a result of a lack of explicit conceptualization and ideological formulation keeping pace with events, the average and official vocabulary conveys the idea that America has accepted the challenge of communism in the very terms of communist propaganda itself: Communism versus Capitalism, America being the stronghold of Capitalism.

That is a great misfortune, it seems to me, with respect to the rest of the world's peoples, for whom capitalism has kept its classical meaning, who loathe the very word, and who are not ready to die for it—nobody is ready to die for capitalism in Asia, Africa, or Europe.

And it is also a great misfortune with respect to the accuracy of language; for the truth is that America is taking leave of capitalism, not through any sudden, violent and destructive revolution, but through steady, constructive—and unsystematic—transmutation.[1]

There are, of course, a number of books, and very

1. "Indeed, to call the American system 'capitalism' is utterly ludicrous, considering what the term means elsewhere . . . The free industrial society that emerges from this analysis is certainly very different from what we have traditionally considered to be 'Capitalism.' It is also very different from what we have considered traditionally

enlightening books, which were written by American authors to stress the truth in question. Here is a list of four of them: Frederick Lewis Allen's *The Big Change,* which I have quoted several times; Adolf Berle's *The 20th Century Capitalist Revolution;* Peter Drucker's *The New Society;* and David Lilienthal's *Big Business: A New Era.*[1]

But all these books were written *after the event.* They offer us reflective analyses of what happened. They were not theoretical elucidations guiding what happened. They did not formulate ideas stirring men's minds and summoning them to action. And they remain so enmeshed in the description of the American experiential process and American particularities that they have a rather limited appeal for those who do not know this country.

In short, they analyze the very first steps in a process which will require at least a century for its full development; whereas that which might arouse the hopes of people all over the world is an idea of the final goal toward which such a process tends.

In actual reality, European scholars who keep

---

to be 'Socialism.' *An industrial society is beyond Capitalism and Socialism. It is a new society transcending both."* Peter F. Drucker, *op. cit.,* pp. 349, 351. (Drucker's italics.)

1. I mention, in addition, another challenging book written from another point of view, and in the perspective of political philosophy, Scott Buchanan's *Essay in Politics.*

themselves well informed on American affairs are aware of the historic fact on which I laid stress; the European masses are completely unaware of it.

You are advancing in the night, bearing torches toward which mankind would be glad to turn; but you leave them enveloped in the fog of a merely experiential approach and mere practical conceptualization, with no universal ideas to communicate. For lack of adequate ideology, your lights cannot be seen.

I think it is too much modesty.

*

This long digression was only an example. It shows us, I think, that this country should never, and will never, give up the experiential approach, which is a blessing for it; but that it would be quite beneficial for it to develop, at the same time, an adequate ideological formulation, an explicit philosophy, expressing its own ideal in communicable terms.

This does not mean, of course, that it would be advisable to manufacture an ideology for the sake of propaganda, God forbid! It means that the development of a greater general interest in ideas and universal verities is a presupposed condition without which no genuine possibilities of intellectual communication can emerge.

For such a function in the community there is need for intellectuals. Here we see how necessary eggheads are—those who try to shed the light of an adequate philosophy and a proper rational formulation, the apostolic power of ideas—if not *ahead* of the movement of life, at least focussed directly upon it, as was the case at the time of the Declaration of Independence and the writing of the Constitution.

Let me insist that at that time America actively shared in the ideological movement which stirred the Western world. She even took the lead in those matters of political philosophy which relate to the Constitution of a free people. It is enough to read *The Federalist* to be certain of the intellectual amplitude of the discussions involved. And such was the role of the American mind in the ideological movement of the day that it had a considerable impact on the French Revolution [1] and the less questionable parts of its philosophy.

1. Cf., in particular, Gilbert Chinard's *Notes on the American Origins of the "Déclaration des Droits de l'Homme et du Citoyen"* (*Proceedings of the American Philosophical Society*, vol. 98, no. 6, December 23, 1954), with the Bibliographical Note, p. 394.

As is well known, the American Declaration of Independence (1776) and the American Constitution (1787) preceded the French *Déclaration* (1789).

The Virginia Declaration of Rights, which was a prelude to the Bill of Rights of the U. S. Constitution, "is older by thirteen years than the French Declaration of the Rights of Man and the Citizen of 1789. Your country can take just pride in being the one where this

Even if under contemporary circumstances the philosophical formulation of a universal ideal seems to be inevitably forestalled by the rush of events, at least it should be possible to bring out from what happened some comprehensive interpretation in terms of social philosophy, and some adequately elaborated systematic program.

————————

historically significant affirmation of human rights was given." Dag Hammarskjold, *The International Significance of the Bill of Rights,* Address delivered in Williamsburg, Virginia, on May 15, 1956.

XIV

The Grand Slander

In a certain detestation and slander of America, there is a sort of mystical ardor and mysterious meaning which is worth examining.

No better expression of this Grand Slander can be found than in the following passages from *The Plumed Serpent*. Speaking of Kate Leslie, the protagonist of the novel, D. H. Lawrence wrote:

"And sometimes she wondered whether America really was the great death-continent, the great No! to the European and Asiatic and even African Yes! Was it really the great melting pot, where men from the creative continents were smelted back again, not to a new creation, but down into the homogeneity of death? Was it the great continent of the undoing, and all its peoples the agents of the mystic destruction! Plucking, plucking at the created soul in a man, till at last it plucked out the growing germ, and left him a creature of mechanism and automatic reaction, with only one inspiration, the desire to pluck the quick out of every living spontaneous creature.

"Was that the clue to America, she sometimes wondered. Was it the great death-continent, the continent that destroyed again what the other continents had built up. The continent whose spirit of place fought purely to pick the eyes out of the face of God. Was that America?

"And all the people who went there, Europeans, Negroes, Japanese, Chinese, all the colours and the races, were they the spent people, in whom the God impulse had collapsed, so they crossed to the great continent of negation, where the human will declares itself 'free' to pull down the soul of the world? Was it so? And did this account for the great drift to the New World, the drift of spent souls passing over to the side of Godless democracy, energetic negation? The negation which is the life-breath of materialism. And would the great negative pull of the Americans at last break the heart of the world?

"This thought would come to her, time and again." [1]

It is obvious enough that, through Kate, Lawrence was expressing his own thoughts and anxieties.[2] In the creative dream, author and character were ambiguously identified. And if they used the inter-

1. D. H. Lawrence, *The Plumed Serpent*, New York: Copyright 1926, 1951 by Alfred A. Knopf, Inc., pp. 73–74.

2. In general "she speaks for Lawrence," William York Tindall writes in his Introduction to the fourth printing (1951), p. ix.

rogative form, and if they ambiguously started from
Mexican hopelessness ("which would pull her down,
pull her down, to the dark depths of nothingness") [1]
to leap at "America" and question "America"—
that is, the great melting pot of industrial America,
the United States—it was because the thought which
haunted them was possessed of the tragic pungency
and equivocity of a daydream. Well, the kind of
testimony that D. H. Lawrence thus bore against
America had all the more remarkable a significance
since the America he loathed was the America, not
only of his own imagination, but also of the imagination of many a man like him, except for the
poetic genius. The very falsity of this furious image
is of special interest to me.

In D. H. Lawrence himself the telling thing, it
seems to me, is the fact that he was devoured by a
profound mystical need, and that he frustrated this
need, turning it toward the experience of the void,
and the maddening negativity of an erotic frenzy
which "declared itself 'free.'" About the ways and
means through which he communed with the mystical realm, Lady Chatterley had surely better information than any of us. In the people for whom
he spoke, however, mystical frustration can take an
infinity of other forms. The new, fresh, life-giving

1. *Ibid.,* p. 72.

paganism of a renovated Quetzalcoatl was only one of the simulacra which can provide such souls with a moment of rapture.

Because they are enraged at themselves they are enraged at man and his daily hopes, sufferings and toil. They are split personalities; they cannot endure what is not torn asunder. It is only normal that they hate everything for which America stands. They are bored to death by such lukewarm, they think, and vulgar ideals as human freedom and human brotherhood. They hate the common people. ("Certainly Kate, who seems most nearly to share Lawrence's attitudes, regards ordinary people with disgust.") [1] They hate those daily tasks and crowded schedules, that struggle and competition, that restless motion of innumerable hands, that pressure of human work —too human for them—toward human, too human ends, and finally toward a life worthy of man for all, which they call energetic negation—and that effort to turn matter to the service of man which they call materialism—and that swarming of all colors and races, that great drift of souls coming over to leave oppression and humiliation behind and to work together in hope and liberty, which they call the great drift of spent souls crossing to the world of the undoing. They hate the spark of Gospel love humbly

1. William York Tindall, Introduction, *op. cit.*, p. ix.

glimmering in a desire to help man against despair.

Then, in order to take revenge upon all those things, and upon their own torment as well, they imagine, in a portentous dream of their own, a purely mechanical inferno which they call America, an America populated only with machines and walking corpses, a *great death continent* where all that they abominate, all that which plucks the quick out of them reigns supreme, which breathes only negation, and whose denatured will is only intent on sucking all the vitality and the creative instinct of the world, in order to foster with them the levelling power of dead matter and a swarm of automatic ghouls. No wonder that they curse this monstrous America of their evil dream as the land of *mystic destruction,* busy pulling down the soul of the world and picking the eyes out of the face of God—of their Plumed God.

*

The fright and horror which haunted D. H. Lawrence's Kate when she thought of America point to a fact which seems to me to be worthy of serious consideration.

Obviously, all over the world businessmen interested in making profits may happen to like America, to learn a great deal from her, and to admire her material activity—they envy her and will never really love her. Obviously, many persons endowed with genuine spirituality may happen to detest and slander America because they don't know her. But the significant thing for me is that I have never met any real contemplative, any true soul of grace, any man genuinely aware of the ways of the spirit, who, knowing America in actual fact and through personal experience, did not have for her a love in which his very love for mankind and a sort of reverence for the workings of divine Providence were involved. Despite all human defects, such as those mentioned in this book, genuine spirituals love America. Her worst enemies are pseudo-spirituals.

America can be slandered and unjustly hated in many various ways. She has political enemies, who foster in her regard a hatred which is violently vociferous but which is a matter of expediency, and can shift to as noisy a fondness and flattery the day it seems tactically advantageous. The natural enemies of America are the pseudo-spirituals, the false witnesses of the spirit. Theirs is the absolute and irreducible, the mystic hatred of America.

This hatred is peculiar to people who look for the divine and are captives of the flesh, and of the void, who thirst for spiritual experience and turn to spurious substitutes for it. It is only in anger and indignation, it is only against someone or something that they can recoup, and bear testimony to the sublimity of the very things they failed to attain. To compensate for their frustration and resentment they need a world-wide scapegoat, a symbolic continent great and powerful enough to arouse mankind's hopes, and perverse enough to betray them— the nightmare [1] of *their* America.

1. "The Air-conditioned Nightmare," as Mr. Henry Miller (who feels like Kate, but has more humor) puts it.

III

XV

Some American Illusions

The illusions I shall point to in this chapter are in no way specifically American. But they seem to me to be not infrequent in this great country; so that their very generality allows me to speak of them as "some American illusions."

Illusion number one. In some respects the American conception of life appears as a continuation of the eighteenth-century optimistic views on Man and Nature.

At first glance it would even seem that this country fosters belief in the goodness of Nature, the natural goodness of Man, in the Rousseauist sense. Everything would be all right if Nature were not repressed, and were left to its own inclinations (without distinguishing between the metaphysical essence of man and the particular nature and existential condition of each one). In other words, there is no hidden root of evil in our nature, no original sin, no need for divine grace. In this way of thinking, which is seemingly accepted here and there but remains quite superficial, and concerns words and the conversational approach more than concepts or any reasoned-out conviction, we have to do with a trend toward naturalism more insidious, I think, than the threat of materialism. The assumption (rather general in our modern world) is that man will attain a state of merely natural perfection and merely natural bliss, and triumph over evil by the sole instrumentality of human energy and human science, and that he is his own Saviour (with the additional guarantee, if you need the solace of religion, of God's approval and encouragement).

Yet there is some serious inconsistency in this very naturalism, because we are confronted with a quite opposite tendency, originating, I think, in a residue of (and bitterness against) old Puritanism.

And from this other point of view Nature is not so good. There is an idea that human nature is fundamentally miserable—a set of brute instincts and desires which clash with each other, and which are not disciplined from within by moral conscience, to be sure, but only repressed from without by social taboos.

As a result, if it were not for the existence of psychologists and engineers, we should say with the

ancient Greeks: it were better for man never to have
been born. . . .

*

Illusion number two. It is generally believed that
success is a thing good in itself, and which it is, from
an ethical point of view, mandatory to strive for.

In this American concept of success there is no
greediness or egoism. It is, it seems to me, rather an
over-simplified idea that "to succeed" is to bear fruit,
and therefore to give proof of the fact that psycho-
logically and morally you are not a failure.

This is a very old illusion, already denounced by
Socrates: mistaking external success, which depends
on a great many ingredients extraneous to ethical
life—good connections, cleverness, good luck, ruthlessness, and so forth—for genuine "success" in the
metaphysical sense, that is, for the genuinely human
happy issue which is internal, and consists in having,
as Socrates said, a "good and beautiful soul."

*

Illusion number three. This is an illusion into
which ethically minded people are liable to fall,
and which boils down to mistaking the part for the
whole.

What I mean is that given a particular objective—for instance, such and such group interest, or business interest, or national interest—which, considered in itself, is, moreover, morally good, some responsible people happen to make this particular good into a universal or an absolute, disregarding the superior and more general good on which, under the circumstances, the rightness of our conduct depends.

Then they believe that what is good for their business or for the particular job with which they are entrusted is good for America, and for mankind. And they believe it *with a perfectly clear conscience* —a fact which enrages more cynical people, who know very well that if *they* had taken the same course of action they would have done so without bothering about any moral justification.

*

Illusion number four. Every professor is liable to meet young men or young women who loathe, in the name of equality, the very notion of any kind of hierarchy—even if it is a question of the degrees of knowledge (it is offensive to say that wisdom is superior to science, or philosophy to chemistry).

*

Illusion number five. Americans seem sometimes

to believe that if you are a thinker you must be a frowning bore, because thinking is so damn serious.

*

Illusion number six. You seem, also, to believe that you don't obey any man—but only law; and that your condition as free men demands that you should be governed not by other men, exercising authority under the law of the land and according to law—but by Law itself, with a capital "L," by an abstract entity which has neither soul nor hands.

*

Illusion number seven. A number of Americans seem to consider that marriage must be both the perfect fulfillment of romantic love and the pursuit of full individual self-realization for the two partners involved.

XVI

Marriage and Happiness

Among the "American illusions" of which I just spoke, the last one—about marriage, romantic love and the pursuit of full individual self-realization— poses, I think, particularly important problems and deserves particular attention.

It is perhaps advisable to try to elucidate the matter a little more by resorting to a few general considerations, and first of all to state more explicitly what I had in mind when I used the expression "romantic love."

To my mind "romantic love" is sexual love when it goes beyond the sphere of simple animality (in which it remains rooted), and bursts into full bloom in the properly human sphere, exalting and ravishing everything in the human being—sentiments, thought, creative activity, which are henceforth imbued with and stimulated by the basic passion of desire.

Such a love carries man beyond himself—in imagination—into a kind of poetical paradise, and makes him believe that he is entirely and eternally dedicated to the one he loves, and that he lives and breathes only for this one, while in reality this other human person is so passionately cherished first of all for the sake of sexual desire and possession, which remain the primary essential incentive.

This romantic love might be defined as a total intoxication of the human being by sexual desire taking the loftiest forms and disguised as pure and absolutely disinterested, pure and eternal love of the other.

Now, since sexual attraction and satisfaction remain the essential incentive and the essential aim, it must be said that romantic love—*l'amour passion* —being but a transcendent human expression of the strongest animal instinct, is, by nature: first, deprived of permanence and liable to fade away; second, unfaithful and liable to shift from one object to another; and third, intrinsically torn between the love for another, which it has awakened, and its own basically egoist nature.

Consequently, to found marriage on romantic love, and to think that marriage must be the perfect fulfillment of romantic love is, as I submitted, a great illusion.

Mankind has been so well aware of this fact that for centuries marriage, being considered a merely social affair, was regarded as a thing with which personal inclination and personal love had nothing—or very little—to do. I am thinking of all those marriages which were arranged by parents, for family interests or tribal considerations—even national interests when it was a question of kings and queens. So that sometimes a boy and a girl had never met one another before they were married.

There was some sad, wicked wisdom in this conception, so far as it recognized the fact that romantic love and married love are two quite different things; and that the aim of marriage is not to bring romantic love to perfect fulfillment.

Yet, in proportion as, in the course of history, the human person became more and more aware of his or her own value and own importance, the merely social conception of marriage to which I just alluded appeared more inhuman and more harmful. For, especially in modern times, a result was that in a number of cases men and women looked for mutual personal love, and romantic love (which is an inherent dream of the human being) outside of marriage. Thus people came to realize that if mutual personal love, and even initially an element of romantic love, are not a necessary requirement of the validity of marriage—at least they are a necessary requirement for its intrinsic dignity and welfare.

Finally, the truth of the matter, as I see it, is, first,

that love as desire or passion, and romantic love— or at least an element of it—should, as far as possible, be present in marriage as a first incentive and starting point. Otherwise, it would be too difficult for the human being, if and when an opportunity for romantic love outside of marriage should later appear, to resist the temptation; for what makes man most unhappy is to be deprived not of that which he had, but of that which he did not have, and did not really know.

The second point is that far from having as its essential aim to bring romantic love to perfect fulfillment, marriage has to perform in human hearts quite another work—an infinitely deeper and more mysterious, alchemical operation: I mean to say, it has to *transmute* romantic love, or what existed of it at the beginning, into real and indestructible *human* love, and really disinterested love, which does not exclude sex, of course, but which grows more and more independent of sex, and even can be, in its highest forms, completely free from sexual desire and intercourse, because it is essentially spiritual in nature—a complete and irrevocable gift of the one to the other, for the sake of the other.

Thus it is that marriage can be between man and woman a true community of love, built not on sand, but on rock, because it is built on genuinely human, not animal, and genuinely spiritual, genuinely *personal* love—through the hard discipline of self-sacrifice and by dint of renouncements and purifications. Then in a free and unceasing ebb and flow of emotion, feeling, and thought, each one really participates, by virtue of love, in that personal life of the other which is, by nature, the other's incommunicable possession. And then each one may become a sort of guardian Angel for the other—prepared, as guardian Angels have to be, to forgive the other a great deal: for the gospel law of mutual forgiveness expresses, I believe, a fundamental requirement which is valid not only in the supernatural order, but in the terrestrial and temporal order as well, and for basically natural societies like domestic society and even political society. Each one, in other words, may then become really dedicated to the good and salvation of the other.

*

After these general considerations, I come now to the American scene. I shall content myself with a brief outline of my subject—I am afraid a whole book would be necessary to attempt a satisfactory study of it.

Speaking of books, there are, from the point of view of rather superficial but witty and valuable ob-

servation, a lot of interesting remarks in a book by
David L. Cohn, *Love in America*,[1] which I remember reading some years ago.

The first thing I would say is that the problem of
the relations between the sexes seems to me to be
still more important, and still more dramatic, in this
country than that of the relations between management and labor, and even that of the relations between races.

Then, I would say that in my opinion American
men and women have undertaken with great courage and good will an attempt to found marriage on
mutual love (more than on considerations of social
standing, clannish interests, expectations of inherit-
ance, and so forth), and to have marriage bring happiness to husband and wife as human persons essentially equal in rights and dignity.

And this is all for the best, indeed, except for the
fact that the attempt in question does not seem to be
largely successful, and that in too many cases good
will ends in unhappiness and conflict: probably, I
think, because there was some fundamental mistake
in the interpretation of the ideal I just alluded to,
and which is quite right in itself but can be understood in a misleading way (if by love one understands

1. New York: Simon and Schuster, 1943.

romantic love, and by happiness, individual self-realization).

My final observation is that the problem of which I am speaking, and which risks making the pursuit of happiness a delusion for so many people, will be successfully solved—so far as in human affairs any solution is possible—when the American mind comes to realize two basic verities.

The first verity is that love is not sex, and that that kind of love on which marriage must be founded is not primarily sensual passion, *l'amour passion,* nor romantic love and that philtre by which Tristan and Isolde were divinely intoxicated—but a deeper and more lasting love, into which, as I said a moment ago, romantic love must be transmuted, and in which sex and passion are but a prime incentive. This deeper and more lasting love takes root and develops at the properly human and spiritual level where the one accepts to be entrusted with the revelation of, and the care for, all that the other *is* in his or her deepest human depths, and where the will is fully dedicated to the good and happiness of the one loved.

The second verity is that if one expects from marriage, in the name of the equal dignity of each one, a final assertion and realization of what one thinks of as one's personality and which is actually no more than self-centered individuality, one prepares for oneself a hell of disappointment and bitterness: because without love, genuinely human love, marriage is a state of servitude, and because love, genuinely human love, is essentially the gift of oneself, that is to say, precisely the opposite of any selfish and self-centered assertion and enjoyment of one's individuality.

As a result, it is through renouncement of such self-realization that real love leads man and woman to a superior form of freedom and happiness, which is purified, and spiritual in nature, and in which the personality of each one is enlarged and uplifted, each one being henceforth primarily centered *in the other,* or having his or her dearest self *in the other.* In contradistinction to love as desire or passion, we have here, I would say, in the etymological sense of the word, love as ecstasy, which makes the human being pass, and exist, outside himself.

I am not suggesting that the two verities I just mentioned are put into practice anywhere in the world more than in this country, or that it is easy to have married life conform to them.

I do suggest that these two verities show us the only way in which it is really possible to make successful the American attempt to found marriage on mutual love only, and have it bring happiness to husband and wife as human persons essentially equal in rights and dignity.

In other words, they express the only true and really human meaning of the ideal after which the American concept of marriage is striving.

XVII

American Openmindedness and Intellectual Courtesy

I have particular admiration for the openminded-ness and intellectual courtesy which are to be found here, and which are characteristic of American culture. Nowhere, I think, is it possible to find such eagerness for everything which appears as genuine research and genuine endeavor to disclose some aspect of truth—an eagerness which is in relation with that thirst for knowledge, that sense of mutual toleration, and respect for human effort, of which I previously spoke. Such vast, encyclopaedic interest in the multifarious aspects of intellectual pioneering is not separated from the typical American interest in man. American people—not only institutions of learning, centers of research, or foundations, but a surprising number of private individuals as well—are anxious to discover men from whom any kind of improvement in the common treasure of the mind may be expected, and to give them a helping hand, so that they can pursue their work in a way profitable for mankind. And all this is done with unequalled thoughtfulness and courtesy.

In some strata of the American population there is, as everybody knows, strong racial bias, and a good deal of religious bias also. Yet what about intellectual bias? My long experience in American life has taught me that there is considerably less intellectual bias and prejudice here than in Europe.

Of course, bitter personal jealousies between scholars, scientists, and professors, not to speak of other vocations, exist here as elsewhere; and even the fact of seeming eccentric, or of appearing too brilliant and aggressive a reformer, or of not "playing the game" according to accepted social rules, is no more forgiven here than elsewhere.

But this fact has to do with community life, with social rules and customs, not with the inner content of the intellectual message a man is conveying. As concerns the proper life and works of the intellect, what I have experienced here is an openmindedness which partakes of the nature of fairness and generosity, and which is a blessing for the general progress of culture.

*

Permit me to take my examples from the field I know best—the field of philosophy.

I am, as you perhaps know, a Thomist philosopher. There was in France, before the war, a strong Thomist movement, but it resulted from the effort of a few rebels who had a talent for crying the truth from the housetops; the steady policy of the official intellectual circles was—and still is—to refuse to recognize even the existence of their work, because nothing, of course, can be expected for philosophy in our times from a man—a theologian! and a saint! —who lived in the thirteenth century.

Now in America, philosophers who hold Thomas Aquinas to be a contemporary thinker are teaching not only in Catholic but in secular universities as well. Here in Chicago we remember some good stories on the matter.[1]

In no European university would I have found the spirit of liberty and congeniality I found at Princeton in teaching moral philosophy in the light of Thomas Aquinas.

1. When I came to Chicago for the first time, in March 1933, Mortimer Adler was teaching Thomist metaphysics in the Law School. And the Department of Philosophy did not like it. As for myself, freshly arrived from Paris at the Institute of Mediaeval Studies of Toronto (a place to which I am particularly indebted, as I am to Etienne Gilson, Dr. Gerald Phelan, and the Basilian Fathers), it was in Chicago that I first met America in the flesh. I had been invited by Robert Hutchins, then President of the University of Chicago, who supported Adler and whose fight against pragmatism was in full bloom; and I gave there my first lecture in English without knowing yet a single word of this language.

Speaking of Princeton, where I am now enjoying the Elysian status of an Emeritus, let me say how indebted I am to President Harold Dodds,[1] and let me indulge, by the same token, in a bit of personal recollection. In December 1947, returning to Rome from Mexico City, I stopped in New York for a few hours to change planes. President Dodds was there; he had been so kind as to come to New York to offer me—if I should resign my diplomatic post at the Vatican—a professorship at Princeton University, precisely in my capacity as a philosopher dedicated to the spirit and principles of Thomas Aquinas. The fact that Princeton is a secular university of Presbyterian origin made him only more interested in such a teaching appointment.

The spirit of liberty of which I am speaking is linked, I think, to the perpetual process of self-criticism and self-improvement which can be observed in small colleges (which are the backbone of your educational system) as in great universities, and in great Catholic universities like the University of Notre Dame as in great secular universities like Princeton or Chicago. I am proud to give regular lectures now both in Notre Dame and Chicago, and at Hunter College too, which is an old friend of mine

1. President Dodds retired in June, 1957; the new President of Princeton University is Dr. Robert Goheen.

—I had the honor of speaking at the inauguration of President George Shuster, on October 10th, 1940 —and where the same spirit of liberty is fostered by this great Christian humanist.

Well, to return to my point after personal digressions (which are, I am afraid, not yet quite finished), the fact is that in philosophical reviews of the most various persuasions it is objectively stated that "neo-Thomism," as they say, is one of the living currents in American philosophy today. The National Society for the Study of Education asked a Thomist philosopher to write a chapter in its Yearbook for 1955, entitled *Modern Philosophies and Education*. (So, according to this Yearbook, Thomism ranks among modern philosophies. Never did M. Emile Bréhier or his colleagues at the Sorbonne recognize the fact.)

All that is a simple matter of intellectual fairness and objectivity.

And let me tell you of another instance, which has for me quite special overtones. There is a great commentator on Thomas Aquinas, John of St. Thomas, who lived in the seventeenth century. He was a dearly loved master and inspirer for me and my friends. But we were quite lonely in our worship of him. The French intellectual circles of which I just spoke were, of course, sublimely ignorant of

him; nay more, among people interested in Thomas
Aquinas a strong majority assumed that they had
sufficiently good eyesight to read the text of the
Summa without any assistance, and they simply
loathed all commentators, and particularly John of
St. Thomas, because of his highly technical and in-
voluted style. Finally, however, it was possible to
have a good edition of his works published in Latin
in France and in Italy; and even a French translation
of his treatise on the gifts of the Holy Spirit, which
is a basic treatise in spiritual life, was published by
my wife. But the very idea of having his logical and
philosophical treatises translated into French (or
into Italian, or German) was inconceivable; and
as a result of the general situation I just described,
he was for our little group a kind of hermetic and
esoteric wise man, whose knowledge was the privilege of the chosen few.

Well, the *Material Logic* of John of St. Thomas,
a book of six hundred and fifty pages, has appeared
in English here, translated by our friend and col-
league Professor Yves Simon and two remarkable
young American scholars.[1] The book was published
by the Chicago University Press, and was given a

1. *The Material Logic of John of St. Thomas, Basic Treatises,* translated by Yves R. Simon, John J. Glanville, G. Donald Hollenhorst,
with a Preface by Jacques Maritain, Chicago: The Chicago University
Press, 1955.

large and most favorable welcome in the philosophical reviews of this country.[1] If it seems today almost
as natural to read John of St. Thomas as to read
Berkeley or Leibnitz, we owe this victory over age-
old prejudices, which we could not even have
dreamed of twenty-five years ago, to the openminded-
ness of American culture.

*

Gratitude is the most exquisite form of courtesy.

America makes life hard for her great men. It is
not, however, in the funeral oration that she is interested, as some other nations are. She puts her
great men to the test, she enjoys seeing them fiercely
attacked by their adversaries, but she loves them,
even before the grave.

And in the ordinary course of life, when simply
men, and not necessarily great men, are involved,
Americans are generous enough not to be afraid to
feel and express gratitude each time they have an
opportunity to do so.

Chateaubriand has a telling sentence: "Les
hommes sont ingrats," he said, "mais l'humanité est

1. The *Summulae* of John of St. Thomas were also published
recently, under the title *Outlines of Formal Logic,* 136 pages, by
Francis C. Wade, S.J., Milwaukee: Marquette University Press, 1955.
(With an interesting essay by the translator on traditional and symbolic logic.)

reconnaissante." Men are ungrateful, but mankind shows gratitude.

Let us say that the distance between man and mankind does not appear so great in this country.

XVIII

Work and Leisure

Many anti-American cartoons abroad depict Uncle Sam brandishing a dollar as a symbol of American civilization. There is more ignorance than malice in this platitude. As a matter of fact, it is not money, it is *work* which holds sway over American civilization.

Everybody is working, and working hard. In this sense all are fundamentally equal, as working people (and people burdened by mortgages and deferred payment systems) who work to make a living, and who, after their daily hours, busy themselves again with any kind of task—handicrafts, improving their houses, sometimes building them, as Dr. Butterfield did, who was so sorry to leave his frame house, entirely built by him, when he became President of Wesleyan University. And they are more proud of their hobbies than of their jobs.

American civilization thus lays stress on the dignity of work and the fecundity of work transforming matter and nature. These are basic verities, in spite of all the fuss that the modern age is making about

155

them—verities that essentially matter to man and society, and which ancient civilizations more or less ignored.

*

Yes. And for all that the fact remains that a certain boredom is caused by the absolute primacy of work and the disregard for the human value of leisure. Here is the dark side of the picture.

Let us think of the American attitude toward time. There is here, it seems to me, a certain horror of any span of time which a man might have at his own disposal in order to *do nothing*. The great value and efficacy of standing idle, and lingering over one's dream, is little appreciated in this country. One might wonder, for instance, whether committee meetings and all similar periodically recurrent administrative nuisances have not been invented to prevent professors, once they have finished lecturing, from having any time for idleness—that is to say, for think· ing at leisure and pursuing their own research.

Well, friendship requires a great waste of time, and much idleness; creative thinking requires a great deal of idleness. So it is that leisure constitutes a serious problem for American life, especially given the social and technical progress, the automation, for instance, which makes working hours shorter and shorter in industry.

The question will be to have leisure time occupied in a manner really profitable to man, and not entirely taken up by the sort of stupefying passivity that is more often than not developed by movies or television. As long as a new cast of mind does not develop, involving a certain amount of spiritual epicureanism, the quality of leisure in the modern world will not be on a level with the quality of work.

If it is true, as Aristotle and Thomas Aquinas thought, that man cannot do without a certain amount of delectation, so that when he is deprived of spiritual delectations he passes over to carnal ones, how be surprised that all over the modern world the mass of humanity tamed by the general boredom of mathematized labor, should, if no superior flame is kindled, naturally become a prey to the obsession of sex (here the phenomenon, while taking especially pedantic forms, mentioned in a previous chapter, has its external or symbolic expression in a curious return to a Greek nostalgia for the figure of Venus).

No leisure time will be enough for man to experience the joys of knowledge, of art and poetry, of devotion to great human causes, of communicating with others in the dreams and anxieties of the mind, of silently conversing with himself and silently conversing with God.

Work, which is a fundamental necessity of our existence, is not an end in itself. We work in order to improve human life. But will this very improvement, in ourselves and in others, only consist in working again and working more? Or will it also consist in the attainment of some superior possession, in which we shall rest? There are many kinds of rest. Laziness is sin. Amusement is good, but less good than work. Certain kinds of repose, in which the mind is supremely active, and reaches, however imperfectly, some fruition of immortality through its contact with truth, or with Eternal Love, are better than work.

Higher forms of leisure are no longer leisure but act come to completion. And the highest form is contemplative activity. *Be still, and know that I am God.*[1]

*

And now, as regards work itself, further considerations may be submitted. The multiplication of technical and artificial facilities for work is intrinsically good, there is no doubt about that. But if these facilities grow at the expense of the natural

1. Psalms, 45:11 (Vulg.)

energies and resourcefulness of individuals, they might result, *per accidens,* in a sort of overcivilization, removing us too far from our native sources and that keenness of instinct which was a privilege of primitive man. The mental habits produced by the mechanization of work impair to some extent the sensitivity and agility of fingers in certain especially delicate manual tasks, and the average American worker, accustomed as he is to following carefully elaborated plans and standard regulations, happens sometimes to shift for himself in unforeseen situations less well than his European fellow worker. I don't deny the fact. I do not believe that the risk implied will ever develop into a serious threat.

Some Americans think that their country, despite the wonderful candor and freshness which are shown by its young people, is rendered older than the Old World by the excess of artificial contrivances and artificial improvements of which it likes to make use. Are they young or old, all these cities where it has become a problem to purchase food products which have not been improved, enriched or energized by a foolish lot of vitamins, proteins, maltose, dextrins, calcium, phosphorus, iron, potassium bicarbonate, milk powder, honey, butter, spices and artificial flavors (fruits are sometimes varnished but not yet injected with anti-histamines or tranquillizers)?

I have never been very much impressed by this line of argumentation. The description just offered was of course slightly exaggerated, for the fun of it. And in general the facilities which art adds to nature only make older, I think, those who have no real youth in themselves. Here, in any case, the instinctive counteraction is not lacking; almost every American dreams of having a farm, and a number of people—not to speak of the farmers themselves—enjoy the real thing. Furthermore one notes, in this highly industrialized country, an amazing fondness for roving about in trailers, breaking new ground, prospecting for the natural riches of the soil, conquering the wilderness, or even leading a solitary life in forests, mountains and lonely spaces.

If it can be said that Americans are not a young people, this is surely not because they like gadgets. The statement is true in quite another sense—in the sense that while they are cheerfully engrossed in building their skyscrapers and their cyclotrons, the age-old experience of the world in misfortune and hard times is secretly flowing back into their hearts, and the unconscious, nocturnal part of their minds is obscurely struggling with all the old dreams, anxieties, and fatigue of mankind, as with haunting ghosts: a revenge that the maliciousness of history is taking on them . . .

XIX

American Lessons in Political and Social Philosophy

This chapter will deal with matters in which, as a philosopher, I am especially interested.

In actual fact, it is in America that I have had a real experience of concrete, existential democracy: not as a set of abstract slogans, or as a lofty ideal, but as an actual, human, working, perpetually tested and perpetually readjusted way of life. Here I met democracy as a living reality. Residing in this country, and observing with lively interest the everyday life of its people, as well as the functioning of its institutions, is a great and illuminating, an unforgettable lesson in political philosophy.

Let me submit a certain number of remarks in this connection.

I. THE COMMUNITY AS GRASS-ROOTS STRUCTURE

My first remark deals with a characteristic which is peculiar to this country, in contradistinction to Europe. We are confronted here with a social struc-

ture which is spontaneously and organically differentiated from its very base—just the opposite of the
false dogma of Jean-Jacques Rousseau, who asserted
that no particular society should be permitted in the
state.

There is in this country a swarming multiplicity
of particular communities—self-organized group-
ings, associations, unions, sodalities, vocational or
religious brotherhoods, in which men join forces
with one another at the elementary level of their
everyday concerns and interests.

At the higher level we see here a plurality of states,
each one with its particular political life and legislation, which have finally grown into a single great
Republic, a single Federal State.

Such basic organic multiplicity, with the tensions
involved, and sometimes a kind of puzzling diversity
which resembles a medieval feature (I am thinking,
for instance, of the diversity from state to state in
the laws regarding daylight saving time), such basic
organic multiplicity is, in my opinion, a particularly
favorable condition for the sound development of
democracy.

Historically, the great fact is that this country
was born of politico-religious communities whose
own autonomous behavior, traditions, and self-gov-
ernment have left an indelible impression on the

general mood of the American people. Hence, at the very time when the necessities of life and the extraordinarily fast growth of the American nation oblige it to increase more and more the powers of the Federal State, the American mind still does not like the look of the very notion of *state*. It feels more comfortable with the notion of *community*.

I understand in the same way the fact that the feelings and instincts of community are much stronger in this country than in Europe (especially in individualistic France), the result of which is a tension, perpetually varying in intensity, between the sense of the community and the sense of individual freedom.

Such tension, to my mind, is normal and fecund in itself. Of course, it happens to create conflicts, especially when the community feels that it is threatened in its very life, and reacts, biologically so to speak, with "posses" which hunt men who are not necessarily criminals. Then a counteraction follows as a rule, in the name of moral tenets such as individual freedom and civil rights, without which the very existence and unity of the nation cannot hold.

Is it true that today the genuine sense of the community has degenerated, in a certain number of people, into what Mr. David Riesman calls the "other-directed" type? I am afraid this sociological category is a little too much of a scientific myth, though the worship of *adjustment to the environment* is sure to be, everywhere in the world, one of the mental diseases of present times. The special dangers it represents for this country must not be underrated. Too many schoolboys and schoolgirls crave to be "popular." Too many individuals are made either sheep-like or miserable by the tyranny of social conformity in suburbs or country towns (and not only there).

*

Pursuing now the considerations with which I began, about the organically differentiated structure of American society, I would like to observe, from the practical point of view, that without that background of differentiated and variegated grouping at the most elementary level of social life, on which I have laid stress, a great social undertaking like the one Saul Alinsky started in Chicago with the Back-of-the-Yards movement, and now the Industrial Areas Foundation—an undertaking which is rooted deeply enough in the people, and whose inspiration is genuine enough, to be able to re-oxygenate the blood of our democracies—would be either impossible or at least very difficult.

In Europe the collective life of the people is both

so atomized and so imbued with politics, so subjugated by political parties, that such an undertaking would require there much longer and more exacting preparatory tilling of the soil. A good friend of mine, who was as enthusiastic as I was about Alinsky's book, *Reveille for Radicals,*[1] and who had accompanied me when I went to Rome as French Ambassador to the Holy See, made every effort to start a similar work in Italy, in order to encourage the people and their various natural leaders, in a particularly needy community in the suburbs of Rome, to awake to their collective problems and to join forces in solving them. For a few weeks it was splendid; he thought he had scored. But very soon everything went to pieces, because the whole business shifted to politics —the only question became which political party would take the upper hand, and reap the moral benefit of the organization.

I must add that in Saul Alinsky's view my friend had put the cart before the horse. He should have begun by stirring up in these atomized communities small local, non-political, grass-roots groups; and only after such groups had functioned for several months should he have attempted to make the community as a whole start a common task. This is the way in which Saul Alinsky himself proceeded, and

1. University of Chicago Press, 1946.

succeeded, with completely unorganized Mexican immigrants in some regions of the United States.

II. THE GREAT POLITICAL ACHIEVEMENT

I come to my second remark. It has to do with the fact that in this country we see the democratic philosophy of life at work in everyday existence. I remember my first impressions in your American cities. I was struck by the fact that I was confronted with no humiliated or servile attitudes, or resentful and aggressive faces.

I know that there is the Bowery and the over-crowded and distressed areas of Harlem in New York, and the slums in Chicago. There are the tramps, there is the sub-proletariat of the "poor whites" in the South and some sections of the Negro population. And, thank God, there are also the hospitality houses founded by Dorothy Day. It is a fact that everywhere in the world the industrial regime tends to make the unorganized or unorganizable individual, the pauper, into the victim of a kind of human sacrifice offered to the gods of civilization. That is the last social disease for mankind to cure by dint of intelligence and generosity everywhere in the world.

But let us return to my remark, which is concerned with the behavior of the average citizen of this country, considered from the point of view of political life.

The average citizen here, whatever his particular vocation may be, appears, as a rule, satisfied to be a man and aware of his basic freedom and dignity as a human being. This basic feeling of personal human dignity is also deep-rooted in the French people. And yet I have come to realize here that the motto of the French Revolution, Liberty, Equality, Fraternity—which can be read even on the front of French prisons (just as in Rome the name of the Holy Spirit is used in connection with a bank, Banco di Santo Spirito)—this motto means in America more than a venerable formula; it corresponds to a general way of thinking which is really at work in the common consciousness and the common existence of the people, and which imparts to the feeling of personal human dignity I just pointed out that kind of assurance which comes from common social recognition.[1]

Let's go a little further. It is the teaching of Aris-

1. "In this country," as I wrote elsewhere, "what is known as the *common man* is neither servile nor arrogant. He has a sense of the dignity of human existence, and he exists in the collective consciousness of the value of each and every man. We have here, in a shape so simply human that pretentious and pedantic people fail to see it clearly, a spiritual gain of infinite price." "America's role in the New Europe," *The Commonweal*, February 26, 1943. In *Pour la Justice*, New York: Maison Française, 1945, p. 224.

totle and Thomas Aquinas (when they speak of the city, the political society, as distinguished from the tribe) that political society is a work of reason and virtue, and implies a will or consent to live together, which freely emanates from the "multitude," or the people.

Well, my point is that nowhere in the world has this notion of the essence of political society been brought into existence more truly than in America.

The American body politic is, I think, the only one which was born independently of the various historical constraints (wars of subjugation, conquests, submission of the conquered to the conquerors, etc.), which in actual fact contributed to create human societies and played so great a part in its own pre-natal conditions. The American body politic is the only one which was fully and explicitly born of free-dom, of the free determination of men to live to-gether and work together at a common task. And in this new political creation, men who belonged to various national stocks and spiritual lineages and religious creeds—and whose ancestors had fought the bitterest battles against one another—have freely willed to live together in peace, as free men under God, pursuing the same temporal and terrestrial common good. Lincoln's phrase about the govern-ment of the people, by the people, and for the people is the best definition of political democracy, and it was but an expression of the concrete, existing reality he dealt with. Furthermore, as regards the aims of American democracy, they cannot be better defined, I think, than by another statement of Abraham Lincoln's—when he spoke, in his First Message, of "the struggle for maintaining in the world that form and substance of government whose leading object is to elevate the condition of men; to lift artificial weights from all shoulders; to clear the paths of laudable pursuit for all; to afford all an unfettered start and a fair chance in the race of life."

I add that the great political achievement of which I am speaking was not only brought about by the forefathers of this country. It is a continuous process of self-creation. And so it is that we can witness here the temporal fellowship of men who have determined to live together by a free choice of their own, in freedom and for freedom; and, consequently, the integration of the new-comers, by virtue of their own free choice, into this terrestrial fellowship in freedom and for freedom. This freedom is not a celestial condition received once and for all, and to be simply enjoyed. Existing in history, and being a human thing—a most precious and lofty, and therefore endangered, human thing in the realm of civilization —it is perpetually threatened by new obstacles and perils arising from new situations in the process of time; and it must be perpetually defended and improved, it must be a new conquest and creation for each generation. It permits of no inertia, no passivity, no rest. It must be unceasingly regenerated by the life-breath of a free people, and so it is one with this very life-breath.

*

The American system is in my opinion the best conceived and the most efficient (at least in the long run) among all existing democratic regimes. For all that, it is neither perfect nor (and this is a proof of its very excellence) made for perfect beings. In order to operate in actual existence, the superior wisdom and lofty principles of the Constitution need the assistance of the less noble stir of human interests and ambitions that the political machines shrewdly elaborate into a kind of political fuel finally available for the progress of the nation. Hence it is that according to witty observers the gratitude of the country should extend not only to the Founding Fathers, but also—far below them—to the "Founding Uncles," [1] whose psychological flair was responsible for the practical mechanisms, tricks and gadgets in

1. Cf. Gerald W. Johnson, "Our Founding Uncles," *The Reporter,* January 17, 1950.

question (such as log-rolling and the "spoils system" for instance).

A particular weak point present in every political regime founded on freedom is the fact that—the people as a whole being unable to keep an eye on each and every force at play in the nation—certain sorts of invisible powers inevitably tend to develop behind the scenes. The "eternal vigilance" exercised by good citizens is the only answer, with the subsequent reforms and readaptations it entails. In America this answer is always sure to be given, sooner or later. But the problem surely exists, nevertheless. It has chronic symptoms, such as the impact exercised on public life by pressure groups and powerful semi-official organizations. For the time being, it seems that its most urgent form has to do with the astonishing growth of corporations.[1]

The weak point I mentioned in the preceding paragraph is common, in one form or another, to all democracies. May I now offer some remarks which are concerned with this country in particular? On the one hand, I think that the American institution of the Supreme Court is one of the great political achievements of modern times, and one of the most significant tributes ever paid to wisdom and its right of pre-eminence in human affairs. Yet, on the other

1. See *supra*, pp. 110–111.

hand, and perhaps because Frenchmen are great admirers, at least in theory, of the principle of the *séparation des pouvoirs,* I am afraid this principle is not always as treasured here as it deserves to be. Let us not speak of the distinction between the executive and the legislative branches of the government—this distinction is impaired in practice to a much greater extent in the French system than in the American one. But a European observer is, I think, inevitably made unhappy by the fact that in America judges [1] and district attorneys [2] are elected by popular vote as are any candidates of a given political party, and have to be successful at the polls —and therefore have to avoid estranging the voters. Does not, moreover, a kind of mingling of the judi-

1. Except in Connecticut, Delaware, Maine, Massachusetts, New Hampshire and New Jersey, where judges are appointed by the chief executive; in South Carolina, Vermont and Virginia, where they are chosen by the legislature; and in Rhode Island, whose trial court judges are appointed by the executive, and Supreme Court judges chosen by the legislature. In Missouri and California judges are selected by the executive but this selection is either corroborated or defeated by popular vote.

Furthermore, in order somehow to lessen the entanglement with politics, sixteen of the thirty-six states whose judiciary is elected at the polls have provisions according to which these elections of judges take place on a more or less nonpartisan basis. (See *Institute of Judicial Administration,* "Selection, Tenure and Removal of Judges," August 10, 1956, 4-U42.)

The members of the Federal judiciary, including those of the Supreme Court, are appointed by the President (confirmation by Congress being always required).

2. Federal district attorneys, who act as deputies of the Attorney-General, are appointed by the executive.

cial and the political take place in other typical instances? As far as I know, a Congressional committee
is not considered to be invested with any judicial
authority, because its final purpose [1] is only to gather
adequate material for legislative work; that is why
it is not subject to the specific rules and guarantees
of the courts; and, nevertheless, being empowered
to investigate the private activities of individuals,
it performs in actual fact a certain number of func-
tions which by their very nature pertain to the judicial realm.[2]

Finally, with regard to some present attitudes of
the people themselves in their political life, there
is probably a good deal of truth in the observations
made recently (that is, at the time when this book
was being completed) by a competent authority on
the matter. "Complacent, prosperous and well fed,"
Adlai Stevenson said, "most of our people want to
also feel secure. They don't want to worry. . . ."
And thus, instead of worrying about the common
good, they prefer to busy themselves "with their new

1. In sound philosophical doctrine, it should be observed at this
point that any human activity is not specified by its end or final
purpose, but by its formal object.

2. The important decision in which the Supreme Court (Watkins
case, June 17, 1957) has assigned proper limits to the power of in-
vestigation of Congressional committees, and stressed the individual
rights of those called to testify, refers to abuses that originated in the
root ambiguity I am pointing to, and which, for a time, obscured in
the eyes of foreign peoples the true traditions of the American nation.

suburban homes and communities. . . ." [1] It has been widely remarked in recent years that—perhaps because they are confronted with world problems apparently too big to be mastered by man—people seem to have, in general, little interest in the dangers involved in a certain trend now developing, whatever the party in power may be, toward conformity and regimentation.

The various criticisms I have just brought up invalidate in no way my praise of the American political system. They only show that this system is human, not angelic; and that, precisely because it is a great human conquest, it demands from men a perpetual effort to surmount its imperfections, and to keep it working, and to keep improving it.

III. IN THE PERSPECTIVE OF "TRUE HUMANISM"

I hope you will pardon me if I seem now to give a more personal turn to my reflections. The fact is that I would like to refer to one of my books, *Humanisme Intégral*,[2] which was published twenty years ago. When I wrote this book, trying to outline a concrete historical ideal suitable to a new Christian

1. Address at Democratic National Conference in San Francisco, *The New York Times,* Feb. 16, 1957.

2. This book was translated into English under the title *True Humanism.* I am pleased neither with this title nor with the translation. One day perhaps a new and better one will be made.

civilization, my perspective was definitely European. I was in no way thinking in American terms, I was thinking especially of France, and of Europe, and of their historical problems, and of the kind of concrete prospective image that might inspire the activity, in the temporal field, of the Catholic youth of my country.

The curious thing in this connection is that, fond as I may have been of America as soon as I saw her, and probably because of the particular perspective in which *Humanisme Intégral* was written, it took a rather long time for me to become aware of the kind of congeniality which existed between what is going on in this country and a number of views I had expressed in my book.

Of course the book is concerned with a concrete historical ideal which is far distant from any present reality. Yet, what matters to me is the *direction* of certain essential trends characteristic of American civilization. And from this point of view I may say that *Humanisme Intégral* appears to me now as a book which had, so to speak, an affinity with the American climate by anticipation.

*

Let me give a few indications in this regard.

First, American society is, at least in the most basic, if not the most complete sense, a classless society. This has nothing to do with the enormous difference in economic welfare and social standing which exists between a few multimillionaires, a number of wealthy ladies and gentlemen, and the huge mass of the population. It has nothing to do, either, with the subtle gamut of social differentiations which depend on family traditions and customs, and make American society really so diversified behind a misleading appearance of uniformity: these differentiations are all the more interesting as they are half-concealed, and only disclosed to persons in the know —through significant nuances in the vocabulary, the dress, the manners; yet they do not interfere with the stream of social inter-communication, and they relate to cultural differences in education and behavior, more than to differences in economic standing.

My point deals with the genuine concept of class, which, as Goetz Briefs has shown in his book on the industrial proletariat,[1] implies in its very definition a certain element of fate or inevitability, I mean the fact that a class, in the proper sense of the word, refers to a social condition which as a rule is hereditary,

1. The French translation of this book appeared under the title *Le Prolétariat Industriel*, Paris: Desclée De Brouwer, 1937, with a preface by me; English translation, *The Proletariat, A Challenge to Western Civilization*, New York and London: McGraw-Hill Book Co., 1937, with a foreword by Horace Taylor.

and to a fixed, solid, relatively immobile social structure: the children of a man and woman who belong to a certain class will also belong to this class; and save for a few accidental exceptions which are but confirmations of the rule, it will be so from generation to generation.

Furthermore, as a result of this fixed social partitioning, a given class mentality, even a given class morality, will develop within each of the social classes in question.

Now, nothing of this nature exists in America, by reason of the kind of fluidity which is peculiar to this country.

On the one hand, there is the well-known fact that everyone is liable to shift from one social position to another; today poor—tomorrow rich—day after tomorrow, penniless again. And this perpetual change is normal, so that there is no hereditary stability in social conditions.

On the other hand, the utmost diversity of social standing exists among the children of any given family. There is a basic inter-communication, a universal mixing of men and ideas. The most various mentalities, owing to national, religious, geographical, professional, environmental factors, are to be found here. There is no class mentality.

We see, thus, in what sense it must be said that

America has brought about in the climate of freedom a classless society. This statement is basically true, as far as the strict sociological concept of class is concerned. But it will become truer in proportion as actual equality of opportunity for each one develops, and as the differences in economic standing become lesser. I am not worried by the fact that some people have too much (I would rather wish that this might be said of everybody). What worries me is the fact that many people don't have enough, even if they are not in dire poverty. Furthermore no society can be called classless in the full sense of the word as long as there are still in it certain areas of dire poverty, or, to put it another way, as long as it does not minister, free of charge, to the absolutely basic needs of human life in each one.

*

Another crucial point relates to the fact that the American economy is now growing beyond capitalism, in the proper, classical sense of this word. I have laid stress on this point in a previous chapter. I shall not discuss it again.

Of course, the "big change" in question will develop in many unforeseeable ways and at the price of unceasing efforts. It will have to gain greater extension and deeper significance. But the thing that matters to me is that this country has discovered the direction in which a new regime, both beyond capitalism and beyond socialism, will gradually take form —a regime which it does not seem inappropriate to describe, as I did in my book, as *personnaliste et communautaire,* personalist and community-minded at the same time.

*

A third point which was emphasized in my book was the pluralist structure of such a society. I need not insist on the congeniality between the pluralist idea and a number of basic features of this country, in which you have a single multi-national state or nation.

*

This pluralism is also to be found in the religious life of America.

Here I come to the last point I wish to make in this section. One of the main themes in *Humanisme Intégral* is the notion of a temporal civilization which is not "sacral" but secular in nature, and in which men belonging to diverse spiritual lineages work together for the terrestrial common good, but which, for all that, is a civilization religiously inspired and vitally Christian in its concrete behavior and morality as a social body.

Now what is in this regard the situation on the American scene?

This situation has been described in a telling fashion by Peter Drucker in his article, "Organized Religion and the American Creed," in the *Review of Politics* of July, 1956.

"The unique relationship," he wrote, "between religion, the state, and society is perhaps the most fundamental—certainly it is the most distinctive—feature of American religious as well as American political life. It is not only central to any understanding of American institutions. It also constitutes the sharpest difference between American and European institutions, concepts, and traditions. This country has developed the most thoroughgoing, if not the only truly secular state . . . The United States is, however, also the only country of the West in which society is conceived as being basically a religious society.

"By its very nature the sphere of the state has to be an autonomous sphere, a sphere entirely of the 'natural reason.' But also, by definition, a free society is only possible if based solidly on the religious individual . . . This leads to the basic American concept: the state must neither support nor favor any one religious denomination. That would be 'establishment,' if not 'prohibition of the free exercise of religion,' and strictly forbidden by the First Amendment to the Constitution. But at the same time the state must always sponsor, protect, and favor religious life in general. The United States is indeed a 'secular' state as far as any one denomination is concerned. But it is at the same time a 'religious' commonwealth as concerns the general belief in the necessity of a truly religious basis of citizenship." [1]

This description of the American situation is clear and plain enough. I shall only add, with respect to my own personal experience, that the first time I heard the President of the United States (it was Franklin Roosevelt) speaking on the radio, address a prayer to God [2]—I realized all of a sudden that the expression "separation between Church and State" does not have, to be sure, the same meaning in French and in American.

I would have been less surprised if I had paid attention to the fact that "the same Congress that wrote the principle of separation of State and Church

1. *Loc. cit.*, pp. 296, 298–299.

2. We know that Lincoln, during the Civil War, proclaimed national days of Fasting, Humiliation and Prayer, the most important of which was the day of April 30, 1863.

into the Constitution in perfectly unambiguous form: 'Congress shall make no law respecting an establishment of religion or prohibiting the free exercise thereof' also established as a matter of course chaplains for both its Houses," [1] and also provided for the appointment and pay of chaplains for the army.

Far beyond the influences received either from Locke or the eighteenth-century Enlightenment, the American Constitution, as I put it in another book, is deep-rooted in the age-old heritage of Christian thought and civilization. "It can be described as an outstanding lay Christian document tinged with the philosophy of the day. The spirit and inspiration of this great political Christian document is basically repugnant to the idea of making human society stand aloof from God and from any religious faith. Thanksgiving and public prayer, the invocation of the name of God at the occasion of any major official gathering, are, in the practical behavior of the nation, a token of this very same spirit and inspiration." [2] The Founding Fathers were neither metaphysicians nor theologians, but their philosophy of life, and their political philosophy, their notion of natural law and of hu-

1. *Ibid.*, p. 298.
2. From *Man and the State,* University of Chicago Press, 1951, pp. 183–184.

man rights, were permeated with concepts worked out by Christian reason and backed up by an unshakeable religious feeling.

So it is that a deep-rooted, sometimes hidden, sometimes unconscious, but actual and alive religious inspiration is embodied in the temporal, secular, lay life of this country; and the very fact does not seem to make those who lack any religious convictions, or who are decidedly atheists, especially uncomfortable—except when the very idea of buses transporting free of charge children educated in denominational schools gives them an intolerable shock.[1]

It is unlikely that, however powerful it may be, the antagonistic trend toward secularism will ever be able to tear away from American civilization the religious inspiration which Peter Drucker's analysis gave us an opportunity to emphasize.

*

These remarks having been made, it must now be said that the necessity for intelligent cooperation between Church and State, apart as their domains may be—a necessity for cooperation which is founded

1. Cf. the controversy about the Supreme Court decision in the Everson case (330 U.S. 1, 1947), and the subsequent outburst of anti-Catholic feelings. The organization known as POAU (Protestants and Other Americans United for the Separation of Church and State) "was formed directly as a result of the Everson decision." Robert F. Drinan, "Everson Case: Ten Years After," *America*, February 9, 1957.

not on mutual will to power but on the service of the common good—has not gained sufficiently explicit recognition in American practice today, especially when it comes to Jefferson's "wall of separation" as understood by the Supreme Court in the McCollum case.[1] And in general, present reality, however significant the four great characteristics I just mentioned, is far from coinciding with the solutions I tried to delineate in *Humanisme Intégral* with respect to the historical ideal fit, in my opinion, for our age of civilization.

Yet the characteristics in question are typical enough to show that nowhere as in this country can we find a state of affairs involving definite though remote possibilities for some conceivable development toward these solutions.

IV. RELIGION AND CIVIL SOCIETY

The religious inspiration which is at work in the temporal consciousness of this country is rooted, of course, in the particular religious creeds to which

1. In the McCollum vs. Board of Education case (333 U.S. 203, 1948) the Supreme Court declared that religious instruction on public school premises was contrary to the Constitution. "The way we have handled the problem in the few cases that have come up so far is nothing to be very proud of," Peter Drucker writes with respect to this *cause célèbre*. "I am convinced that it is a thoroughly untenable decision on ordinary legal grounds alone." *Loc. cit.*, pp. 301–302.

such or such individuals or families subscribe, and which, so far as the life of souls is concerned, pertain to the spiritual order. But this same religious inspiration, so far as the collective behavior of the nation is concerned, appears rather as a projection of religious belief *into the temporal order*—a temporal projection of religious belief which holds, in actual fact, for a number of individuals who have slipped away from religious faith, though it can obviously preserve its vitality only if in many others it is not cut off from living religious faith.

Furthermore, thanks to the spirit of fellowship and mutual toleration on which I laid stress previously, this inspiration is compatible with the multiplicity of religious denominations which can be seen here, and with the tensions between religious groups, which are revealed now and then on the American scene.

The aspect I am speaking of has been made very clear in a recent book (Will Herberg's *Protestant, Catholic, Jew*) [1] which gives a remarkable account

1. New York: Doubleday, 1955. From the numerical point of view the Jewish denomination represents a small minority in comparison with the Protestant and Catholic denominations. But this fact does not prevent the Jews from playing an essential and indispensable part, as a dynamic ferment, in American life.

The mutual ties between the Jewish mind and the American mind were rightly stressed in a collective letter written apropos of the State of Israel and signed by a number of influential American per-of the basic religious pluralism in American life, and, at the same time, shows how this pluralism remains encompassed within the single framework of the Judaeo-Christian tradition.

Now, just as it is not particularly favorable, as a rule, for religion to be too much brandished about and made use of by the officials of any government, so the much deeper phenomenon of which I just spoke—temporalized religious inspiration in a nation or a civilization—however normal and salutary it may be in itself, involves its own accidental dangers. The risk is that *religion itself* might become

sonalities (*The New York Times*, February 3, 1957). I quote from this letter:

"One of the first characteristics of our country is that we are a nation of immigrants who have attained unity in seeking a common goal. Israel, in opening its door to 800,000 immigrants from seventy-two nations in the past eight and a half years, has re-enacted our own earlier history.

"Our United States is proud that we are a nation of many origins. We are also proud of being a pioneer people and of still cherishing the pioneer spirit. Israel, in its small area, is carrying on what could be called intensive pioneering; exploring and developing what seemed limited resources with the same imagination that enabled our ancestors to develop far larger and more obvious ones.

"Americans literally have died to establish a democratic equality of opportunity within a republican frame of government. Israelis have shown the same devotion to that ideal.

"Long ago we in the United States committed ourselves to the concept of protection of individual dignity. Just so have the Israelis established laws to defend civil and religious rights, with a Supreme Court, modeled on our own, as a strong bulwark of those liberties."

temporalized, in other words, so institutionalized in the temporal structures themselves and the temporal growth itself of a given civilization, that it would practically lose its essential supernatural, supra-temporal, and supra-national transcendence, and become subservient to particular national or temporal interests.

As Miss Barbara Ward rightly puts it, "It is . . . one thing to argue that a recovery of faith in God is necessary as a safeguard of Western freedom. It is quite another to put forward sociological and political and historical facts as the basis for a revival of faith. . . . Faith is not a matter of convenience nor even—save indirectly—a matter of sociology . . . Faith will not be restored in the West because people believe it to be useful. It will return only when they find that it is true." [1] In other words, we do not need a faith to live by; we need a faith to live for, and if necessary, to die for.

Let us say, then, that any temporalized religious inspiration runs the risk of terminating in a failure if religion in its own order does not victoriously resist any trend toward becoming itself temporalized, that is to say, if, in the inner realm of human souls,

1. Barbara Ward, *Faith and Freedom*, New York: W. W. Norton, 1954, p. 265; London: Hamish Hamilton, Ltd., 1954.

faith in supernatural Truth and obedience to the law of God, the fire of true love and the life of divine grace are not steadily growing.

*

To say that a nation is religiously inspired is in no way to assert that this inspiration is as deep and as decisive as it should be. There is a long way from the present state of affairs, anywhere in the world, to a civilization vitally Christian in the full sense of the word, and to the ideal, even relative to a given age in human history, of a genuinely Christian-inspired civilization.

But what matters, when it comes to an appreciation of our present times, are the possibilities for the future which exist in our day.

From this point of view we may believe that if a new Christian civilization, a new Christendom is ever to come about in human history, it is on American soil that it will find its starting point.

Then, the Atlantic Ocean would become the great inner lake of Western civilization, as the Mediterranean Sea was for classical antiquity. And then, perhaps, the old Christian vocation of France,[1] for

1. I mean the Christian vocation of France as a nation, and in the temporal and cultural sphere. As for French Catholics, they have never fallen short of their vocation as pioneers in the spiritual field of apostolic work and self-sacrifice.

which, despite misfortune and disillusionment, Frenchmen will always yearn, would revive at the contact of the Christian vocation of America, and grow in association with it.

On the question of a new Christian civilization I would like to make my thought completely clear.

I am far from saying that today's American civilization *is* a new Christendom, even in outline. It is rather a combination of certain continuing elements of ancient Christian civilization with new temporal achievements and new historical situations.

I do say that today's American civilization *may become* a soil particularly propitious for the development of a new Christendom, if the spark flies and a spiritual renewal takes place in souls strong enough to reverse the trend toward naturalism mentioned in a previous chapter, and to make Christian faith and morality actually prevail in the common consciousness and common behavior; and if such a spiritual renewal is also strong enough to express itself in public life, so that, to begin with, Christian justice would make prejudice and inequity toward colored people definitely disappear, and, in the face of modern war with its devilish weapons, Christian wisdom would succeed in making obedience to moral imperatives and to the law of God dominate over all other considerations, and would discover a way to bring the threat of atomic warfare to an end.

Now I seem to hear somebody ask me: how can you have the face to speak of a new Christendom to come, when you see the state of our present world, with all the threats of degradation and even destruction to which mankind is being subjected, and had you not better speak of new barbarism already come?

Well, a three-fold answer is possible.

First: history is ambivalent. At the very same time that evil seems to grow triumphant, the ferment of justice and the energies of renewal are more or less secretly making headway and quickening the movement of mankind. At each epoch of history the world was in a hopeless state, and at each epoch of history the world muddled through; at each epoch the world was lost, and at each epoch it was saved.

Second: a new Christendom is possible to the very extent to which faith in Christ is actually alive among men. And despite the progress of absolute atheism (this at least has unmasked the hypocrisy which sheltered anthropocentric humanism's [1] practical contempt for God) not only is faith in Christ still alive, but it is bolder—and more intent on understanding and transforming the temporal realm

---

1. In contradistinction to theocentric humanism, which is, I believe, the sort of humanism especially needed by our age.

of civilization—in contemporary man than it was in the man of the nineteenth century.

Third: a new Christendom is not only possible, it is also a focus toward which all really progressive energies at work in history since the disintegration of the Middle Ages have actually been tending. There are other forces, working in the opposite direction. It is on human freedom that the issue depends.

And now, if these answers are not accepted, what can I do? I shall say: I believe in the possible advent of a new Christendom because my name is Jacques. Peter typified faith, and John charity; James typified the second theological virtue.

I expect Saints and Miracle-workers to arise in the midst of the labors of the world. Without them I have no idea how a new Christian civilization can ever come about.

XX

America Is Promise

Given the contingency of matter and the free will of men, there are, at each moment of history, always two possible different directions open regarding the future.

Thus there is a possibility that in the course of centuries America may become *embourgeoisée*—a nation interested only in its own material welfare and power. The realization of such a possibility is, to my mind, improbable. The obvious fact is that America is not a nation like others; and she will not become so as long as she remains true to the specific, original impulse and spirit by virtue of which she was born.

Her true future, I said a moment ago, lies in the task of somehow clearing the way for a new Christian civilization. If such an undertaking takes place, it will be a common undertaking. It can be accomplished only in cooperation with all the nations that are stirred by the Christian ferment. (And, no doubt, those Christians who are now the "silent Church" and suffer persecution behind the Iron Curtain will have in this connection particularly great lessons to teach the world, if and when they can speak out freely.) In his remarkable book, *The United States and Civilization*,[1] so genuinely American both in its generous inspiration and its soul-searching self-criticism, John Nef has rightly emphasized the universally human character of the endeavor to which we are called today. Quite significant in this regard, and with respect to the supra-national spirit which is now more necessary than ever, is the appeal with which the author terminates his book, paraphrasing two famous passages from Rousseau and Marx: "Goodness and wisdom were born free, but everywhere they are in chains. Good people, honorable people, intelligent people, truth-loving people of the world, unite. You have nothing material to gain for yourselves; but you have the opportunity to serve humanity. You have the opportunity to bring about a rebirth of the human mind and spirit."

*

It is not irrelevant to say again, at this point, what I said in 1943: "There is indeed one thing that Europe knows well, and knows only too well; that is

1. University of Chicago Press, 1942.

the tragic significance of life. . . . There is one thing
that America knows well, and that she teaches as a
great and precious lesson to those who come in
contact with her astounding adventure: it is the
value and dignity of the common man, the value
and dignity of the people . . . America knows that
the common man has a right to the 'pursuit of happiness'; the pursuit of the elementary conditions and
possessions which are the prerequisites of a free life,
and the denial of which, suffered by such multitudes,
is a horrible wound in the flesh of humanity; the
pursuit of the higher possessions of culture and the
spirit. . . . Here heroism is required, not to overcome tragedy, but to bring to a successful conclusion
the formidable adventure begun in this country
with the Pilgrim Fathers and the pioneers, and
continued in the great days of the Declaration of
Independence and the Revolutionary War.

"No lasting good can be done to the world if the
sense of the tragedy of life, and that quality of
heroism which Europe must display to overcome its
tragedy, and the sense of the great human adventure,
and that quality of heroism which America must display to lead her adventure to completion, are not
joined with one another in boldness and faith. . . .

"It will be necessary for the European spirit and

the American spirit to meet and cooperate in common good will. We do not believe that Paradise will be reached tomorrow. But the task to which we are summoned, the work we will have to pursue, with all the more courage and hope as it will be incessantly betrayed by human weakness, must have as its aim, if we want civilization to survive, a world of free men penetrated in its secular substance by a real and vital Christianity, a world in which the inspiration of the Gospel will direct the common life of man toward an heroic humanism." [1]

*

There is no place in the world where Christian philosophy is more needed and has better opportunities than in this country.

*

The great and admirable strength of America consists in this, that America *is* truly the American people.

*

I have laid stress on the crucial change which took

1. "America's Role in the New Europe," *The Commonweal*, February 26, 1943, Vol. XXXVII, No. 19. In *Pour la Justice*, New York: Maison Française, 1945, pp. 224–227.

place in the American economic and social regime under the steady, unsystematic pressure of the spirit of the people, stronger than the logic of the structure, considered in its material components, of the industrial system.

The inner transformation through which corporations are becoming aware of the primacy of human welfare and the political common good must not be looked at separately from the growing power of organized labor and its growing sense, too, of the primacy of the general welfare and the political common good. These two phenomena taken together are great signs foreshadowing a new age in the development of democratic societies. But big corporations, even when they have "obtained intelligence"— in default of a soul—are surely not enough to herald a new Christian civilization. The same must be said of organized labor power. Intelligent collective self-interest remains very far indeed from anything resembling such an ideal.

Both socially minded corporations and socially minded labor are but laying necessary pre-conditions for any possible start toward the ideal in question. The decisive factor is the spiritual one, and the decisive question is whether the genuine spirit of the Judaeo-Christian tradition will be able to take the lead.

There is matter for fruitful meditation in the last two pages of Adolf Berle's previously quoted book: "In ascending scale," the author says, "is the fact that so long as speech and thought are free, men will always rise capable of transcending the massed effects of any organization or group of organizations. There is solid ground for the expectation that twenty years from now the men of greatest renown in the United States will be the spiritual, philosophical, and intellectual leaders for the sufficient reason that they will be needed more than any other type of men. Society still tends to produce and to honor the kinds of men it needs most.

"We have noted that priests have usually been able to intimidate the policemen, and that philosophers can usually check the politicians. There is fair historical ground to anticipate that moral and intellectual leadership will appear capable of balancing our Frankenstein creations. Men working in that range are measurably steeled to resist normal pressures and often free from normal fears. They frequently have a rough time on the way. It is no accident that some of the greatest saints in the Christian Calendar were non-conformist deviants in their time; but they still grasp the future with their conceptions.

"These, I think, are the real builders of any 'City
of God' Americans would come to accept." [1]

*

"America was Promises"—that is the title of a
beautiful poem by Archibald MacLeish. From the
very beginning the European peoples dreamed of
America as the Fortunate Isles, the land of promise
here below. America can give them goods, food,
industrial equipment. They will take them, of
course, but they will never be content with them,
and never be grateful to America for them.

What they expect from America is: Hope. And
please God that this crucial fact may never be forgotten here.

It is possible to be more specific, and to say: what
the world expects from America is that she keep
alive, in human history, a fraternal recognition of
the dignity of man—in other words, the terrestrial
hope of men in the Gospel.

*

Of course, we always tend to see those we love in
the light of our own dreams and our own hopes. I
trust, nevertheless, that my random reflections, sub-

1. Adolf Berle, *op. cit.*, pp. 187–188.

jective as they may be, are truer than many a study conceived in merely statistical terms. There are, moreover, a great number of aspects, even important aspects, in the American scene which I have not touched upon. Random reflections may indeed be unending, but the patience of the reader has an end.

INDEX OF NAMES

INDEX OF NAMES

Index

Index

GARY LIBRARY
VERMONT COLLEGE

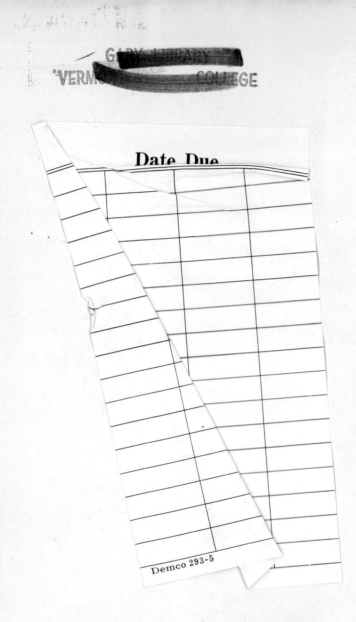

Date Due

Demco 293-5